Mel Bay's Modern
CLASSICAL
GUITAR METHOD
GRADE 1

by Stanley Yates

CD Contents

An instructional DVD containing demonstrations, practice tips and performances of many of the exercises, studies and solos contained in this book is also available. Order MB21548DVD at www.MELBAY.com.

1 2 3 4 5 6 7 8 9 0

Visit us on the Web at www.melbay.com — E-mail us at email@melbay.com

The Classical Guitar

Welcome to the *Mel Bay Modern Classical Guitar Method!*

The fact that you're reading this suggests you've already developed an interest in the classical guitar, so let's look a little more closely into what the term "classical guitar" actually means.

The classical guitar is an instrument that arrived at its present form over a period of almost five-hundred years of development—it's earliest surviving music dates from 16th-century Spain. Since that time, the guitar has experienced periods of considerable popularity. A second "Golden Age" occurred during the Baroque period (c.1600-1730), the guitar being a favored instrument at many European royal courts (including that of the "Sun King," Louise XIV at Versailles). A further period of popularity occurred at the end of the Classical period (c.1800), with many freelance guitar composers successfully competing in the musical salons of the principal European musical centers, Paris and Vienna (Empress Josephine, wife of Napoleon Bonaparte, was a patron of the guitar). Interest in the classical guitar reached an unprecedented level during the early 20th century through the recordings and concert tours of Spanish guitarist Andres Segovia—a guitarist who inspired many important composers to write music for the guitar and who brought the instrument to the same venues and audiences enjoyed by mainstream classical music instruments such as the violin and the piano. Today, the classical guitar is heard in the world's major concert halls, is taught in the world's major music conservatories, and has music written for it by most of today's leading composers.

The term "classical guitar" also refers to a style of guitar construction. For example, the classical guitar neck is wider than those of other types of guitar (almost all of which were originally intended to be played with a pick rather than with the right-hand fingers)—this allows plenty of room for the fingers of both hands to maneuver between the strings. The strings themselves are another distinguishing feature—unlike other types of guitar, the classical guitar uses nylon strings, rather than steel. (In the days before nylon—before around 1945—classical guitarists used strings made of animal gut!). Nylon strings are lower in tension than steel strings, and classical guitars are constructed with this in mind. The resulting sound is warm and velvety but also quite variable in tone quality and volume. Control over sound quality and volume is one of the classical guitarist's most important skills.

The term classical guitar also indicates a playing technique in which all the fingers of both hands are used equally. By using all the fingers, the classical guitarist is able to play solo pieces that present both melody and accompaniment at the same time. The playing technique developed through classical guitar study can of course be useful to steel-string acoustic *(fingerstyle)* guitarists and electric guitarists as well.

This Book and How to Use It

The main difficulty in writing a useful classical guitar method lies in the communication of information to a diverse target audience: self-teachers, teachers whose specialization may not be classical guitar, experienced specialist classical guitar teachers, students whose interests are purely recreational, and students who may ultimately go on to become professional guitarists themselves. A useful classical guitar method must address, in a balanced way, the interests of all of these potential users, and this has been an important consideration in my approach to writing this method.

The opening sections of this book address issues that must be taken into account before any real playing can take place: hand positions, playing position, counting musical time, music notation, and so on. Students studying with a teacher (which is highly recommended!) will undoubtedly go through all of this material quickly, during the first lesson or two. Self-teachers, however, will need to make a careful reading of this material for themselves before proceeding to the actual musical exercises.

Experienced teachers will surely notice that the pedagogical sequence of this book is not the usual one. Since rhythm is *the* fundamental musical skill, I begin with simple strummed chords. I follow this with plucked notes with the thumb, plucked chords with the thumb alternating with the right-hand fingers together, and simple arpeggios—I believe that fluid right-hand technique is built on arpeggio technique rather than melodic playing (especially regarding hand-position) and that this should be fully assimilated before melodic playing is introduced. From this point, the method progresses through an integrated mixture of melodic and arpeggio techniques. For similar reasons, rest-stroke technique is not recommended for the initial stages of study and I suggest it not be used for any of the material in this book.

The guitar is a "right-handed instrument," and I believe that the right hand must be fundamentally secure before the left hand can be developed. Consequently, left-hand activity has been kept to a minimum in this first volume.

The study of a musical instrument can lead to a lifetime of enjoyment and discovery. I wish all who use this book the rewards and fulfillment that I and my fellow classical guitarists—professional and recreational alike—have derived from our study of the classical guitar and its music.

I hope this method will be useful to all who may use it!

The CD and DVD
All of the teacher accompaniments and most of the student exercises and solos are included on the CD that accompanies this book. This should be useful not only for self-teachers but also for students practicing outside of lessons who do have a teacher. Teacher accompaniments are placed on the left stereo channel, student parts on the right. A detailed track list is provided at the end of this book.

The DVD produced in conjunction with this book provides much information that cannot possibly be fully communicated with words alone and should be of considerable help to self-teachers and those teachers whose primary focus is other than the classical guitar.

Thanks
I am indebted to Mir Ali, Denise Cohen, Douglas James, Karl Wohlwend and, in particular, Stephen Aron for their valuable suggestions during the final draft stages of this book. I would also like to thank William Bay for inviting me to contribute to Mel Bay Publication's outstanding catalogue of instructional materials.

Stanley Yates

Parts of the Guitar

Here are the parts of the classical guitar you need to be familiar with:

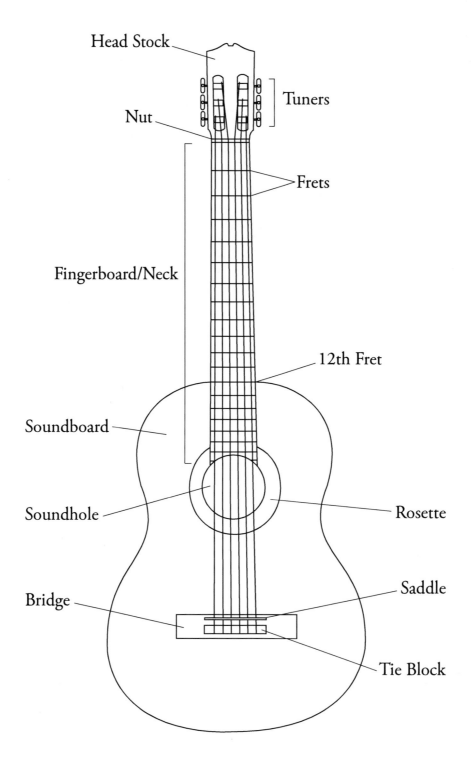

Though concert guitars are made today in a fairly standardized size, it is possible to obtain smaller instruments for younger students or for people with smaller hands, ranging from slightly smaller to three-quarter-size instruments.

Playability

While it's fairly easy to find decent instruments at reasonable prices, students can find themselves in the position of having obtained an instrument that is difficult to play. The main thing to look for is the distance between the strings and the top of the frets—the *action*:

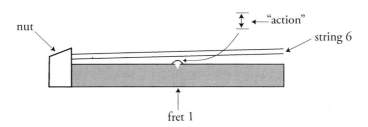

Classical guitars do require a slightly higher action than electric and steel-string acoustic guitars, but if the action is too high playing becomes difficult for the left hand. Although the action is meant to get higher as we move up the fingerboard from the lower frets to the higher ones, it should not become excessive. If the action is too low, on the other hand, the strings will rattle against the frets when plucked strongly.[1]

Replacing Strings

Over time (several months) guitar strings become worn and lose their tonal qualities. It then becomes necessary to replace them. When it's time to replace the strings replace all of them, not simply the ones that appear most worn. As a beginner, you should use "normal" tension strings rather than the "hard" or "extra-hard" tension sets that many professional players prefer. You should also be sure to use nylon "classical guitar strings" rather than any type of steel strings—the higher tension of steel strings could damage your guitar.

Replacing classical guitar strings can be a bit tricky due to the way the knots need to be tied at the bridge and at the rollers (tuners). Here's a common method of tying the knots:

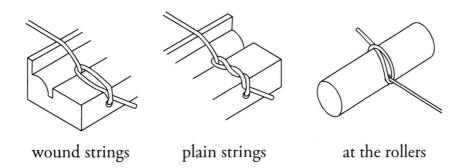

wound strings   plain strings   at the rollers

Several Internet sites provide detailed illustrations and step-by-step instructions on how to re-string a classical guitar.

---

1   The following distances are recommended (you may need to take your guitar to a music store or guitar repair specialist to have this checked properly and adjusted if necessary):

At the first fret:
string 6 = 0.7mm
string 1 = 0.5mm
At fret 12:
string 6 (with the string held down at the first fret) = 3-4mm
string 1 (with the string held down at the first fret) = 2-3mm

Finger Names and Numbers

Standardized names and numbers are used to identify the fingers of the two hands:

> The right-hand fingers are named **p** (thumb), **i** (index), **m** (middle), **a** (ring) and **c** (little)—these are abbreviated versions of the original Spanish, French and Italian names for the fingers.
>
> The left-hand fingers are identified by numbers: **1** (index), **2** (middle), **3** (ring) and **4** (little).

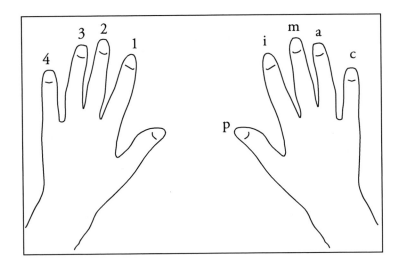

NOTE: almost all classical guitarists use the right-hand fingernails to pluck the strings. However, it is recommended that beginners at first play without nails. Information on filing and plucking with the nails is provided later (on pages 37-38).

String Numbers

The six strings of the guitar are numbered 1-6, from thinnest to thickest, and in musical notation are circled to distinguish them from left-hand finger numbers.[1] The three thinner strings (the plain nylon strings) are referred to as the *trebles*; the thicker (wound) strings are referred to as the *basses*.

The note-names associated with the six open-strings should be memorized:

① — **E**   ④ — **D**
② — **B**   ⑤ — **A**
③ — **G**   ⑥ — **E**

---

1   Guitarists often refer to string ① as the "top string" and string ⑥ as the "bottom string," referring not to the physical position of those strings on the guitar (which is actually the reverse) but to their *pitch* (see page 23).

Sitting Position

Although it might seem a bit fussy to describe a specific sitting position for playing the guitar, it is important to develop a consistent position that promotes the best use of the hands.

The guitar is positioned so as to allow the hands to play in the easiest, most effective way. This means that the guitar neck should point upwards, and this is the reason that classical guitarists use a footstool (or other device) to help position the guitar:

- Sit up straight (use a chair without arms).

- Keep the shoulders relaxed and level with one another.

- The guitar head-stock is approximately at eye level.

- The footstool is positioned such that the left leg does not stick out to the side.

- The right leg moves away to the side.

- The guitar does not stick out to the player's left (the soundhole is directly beneath the chin).

- The right arm rests on the top edge of the guitar at a point approximately in line with the bridge.

Although you can't see this in the previous diagram, there are a couple of further things to consider:

- The guitar head-stock should point slightly forward (the left arm reaches forward a little to reach the fingerboard while the shoulders remain level).

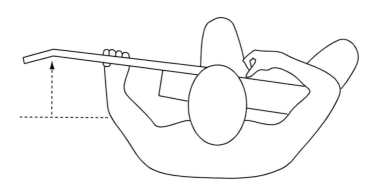

- The guitar is tilted back *a little* (which helps the left hand fret its notes and allows the player to see the fingerboard without leaning forward).

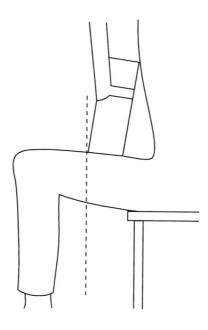

The left hand should not be used to hold the guitar in position during actual playing. The weight of the right arm resting on the top edge of the guitar and the contact of the guitar with the legs and the chest is all that is needed to keep the guitar stable.

Right-Hand Position

The playing positions of both hands are based on a loose fist. To form the right-hand position, make a fist with the thumb held against the side of the index finger and gently relax the fist out so the fingers are gently curved in all their joints. The fingers should be lightly touching each other at the tip joints.

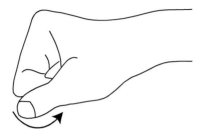 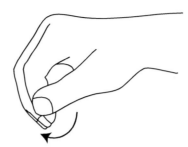

Once this position is established, place the underside of the forearm on the top edge of the guitar (a few inches from the elbow, approximately at the point where the bridge would meet the edge of the guitar). Place the thumb on string ⑥ and the *i, m* and *a* fingers on strings ③, ② and ① respectively, approximately over the rosette. The wrist should have a gentle arch and should not be bent to one side or the other.

Seen from the front, the fingers approach the strings at an angle:

The thumb also forms an angle relative to the strings as seen from above, as the player sees it:

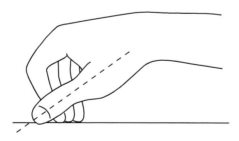

Remember, quickly flexing followed by slowly relaxing a fist is a sure way to place the finger joints in the correct position.

Check the position of the thumb by strumming across the six strings, simply moving the arm from the elbow (and keeping the fingers curled). (Avoid resting any of the fingers on the top of the guitar.)

The Left Hand

Starting out with the left arm hanging loosely by your side, bend your arm at the elbow to bring the hand toward the strings around the fifth fret. Take care not to tense the shoulder. Before actually placing the fingers on the strings, make and gently relax a fist—open the fist just enough to allow the guitar neck to slot in between the fingers and thumb.

Lightly rest the fingers on the fourth string and *lightly* rest the thumb on the back of the guitar neck.

The position of the thumb is important. If the thumb could pass through the wood of the guitar neck, it would come to rest against the tips of the first and second fingers. A good way to check if the thumb is positioned correctly is to simply move it away from the guitar neck and put it back again.

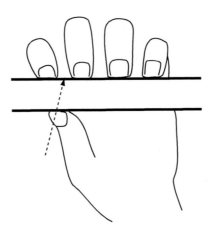

The position of the thumb relatively higher or lower on the guitar neck is also important. If the thumb is positioned too close to the bottom edge of the guitar neck, the wrist will become bent and the fingers will straighten. If the thumb is positioned too close to the upper edge of the guitar neck, the wrist will bend backwards on itself and the fingers will curl too tightly.

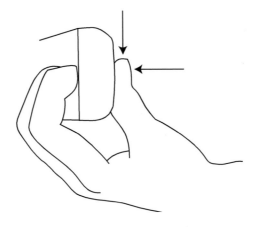

Finally, the thumb should not be allowed to come over or "hang-on" to the top edge of the guitar neck. Although electric guitarists and steel-string guitarists often use the thumb this way, the fingerboard of a classical guitar is too wide for the thumb to be able to do this without hampering the position of the fingers.

This probably all sounds a bit involved, but it is important to establish correct hand positions from the beginning of your studies.

Daily Left-Hand Exercises

The guitarist's left hand is quite gymnastic, constantly moving along and across the fingerboard and adopting all kinds of finger dispositions as it does so. To help develop the necessary coordination and touch of the fingers, a few minutes should be spent each day on specific left-hand exercises. These are the kind of exercises professional guitarists continue to practice. They're not intended to be mastered right away but are "work in progress."

Here are a few things to try:

- Rest the four left-hand fingers on string ④ with the first finger at fret 5 and the other fingers on frets 6, 7 and 8 (it might be easier for you to establish this position by placing the fourth finger first and working backwards to the first finger). Because the first finger is positioned at fret 5, this is referred to as the *fifth position*. Check to make sure the thumb is relaxed and is resting gently against the back of the guitar neck.

- Slowly lift and replace all four fingers together a few times. Can you do this without any of the fingers flying away from the others?

- Next, after placing the four fingers on the string, slowly lift and replace each finger a few times, leaving the others down on the string. Can you lift and replace each finger without any of the others moving?

- Prepare the four fingers on the string and then lift them off a short distance. Slowly add the fingers to the string in the following sequence: 1-2-3-4. Can you do this without the fourth finger flying away as you place fingers two and three?

- Finally (and quite a bit trickier), with the four fingers on the string, slowly lift each finger in the following sequence: 4-3-2-1. Can you keep the fourth finger close to the string as you lift fingers three and two?

Remember, these exercises are work in progress—practice them for a few minutes each day and your finger control will develop.

NOTE: the left-hand fingernails should be kept short. Otherwise, it becomes impossible to accurately fret notes with the fingertips.

Minimum Pressure Exercise

It is important to avoid pressing the strings with any more pressure than is necessary and it is also important to position the fingers as close to the frets as possible (though not directly on top of them):

Use the following routine to discover exactly how much (actually, how little) pressure you need:

- Lightly rest the first finger on string ④ at fret 5 (but don't press down yet). Make sure the finger is positioned just to the side of the metal fret.

- Slowly and repeatedly pluck the string with your thumb, and gradually increase the pressure with the first finger.

- At first, you will hear only a dull thud.

- As you gradually increase the pressure, the string will begin to rattle against the fret.

- A little more pressure and the note will sound clearly.

Repeat the exercise but with the finger positioned about 1/2 an inch further back from the fret:

How does this effect the amount of pressure you need to produce a clear note ?

This should illustrate the importance of placing the fingers close to the frets. Try this exercise with any finger on any string at any fret (try a few different ones each day).

Moving Around the Fingerboard

Having established the basic left-hand position it's simply a matter of keeping the fingers in the same "shape" as you move around (across or along) the fingerboard. In other words, the arm moves and carries the hand and fingers to their new position.

To practice moving across the fingerboard to a new string, use the following routine:

- Start with the fingers resting on string ④ in the fifth position (the first finger at fret 5).

- Lift the fingers together and release the thumb a short distance from the guitar neck.

- Move the arm downwards (towards the floor) to carry the hand and fingers to the next string (string ③); the fingers themselves do not change their curvature or shape. (Note: the fingers *do* straighten a little to play on string ⑥ and curl a little more to play on string ①.)

- Place the fingers on string ③ and the place thumb back on the guitar neck (at the same time).

- Practice in the same way, moving between various pairs of strings.

Use the following routine to practice moving along the fingerboard:

- Start with the fingers resting on string ④ in the fifth position.

- Lift the fingers together and release the thumb.

- Move your arm toward your body to carry the hand and fingers along the string by one fret to the next position (the first finger at fret 6—*the sixth position*); again, the fingers themselves do not change their curvature or shape.

- Place the fingers back on the string in the new position and, at the same time, place the thumb back on the guitar neck.

- Practice in the same way, moving along the strings to various positions along the fingerboard.

Tone Color

You might also wish to explore some of the tone contrasts available on the classical guitar by plucking with the thumb at different points along the string. The normal sound of the guitar is obtained by plucking at the edge of the soundhole, approximately over the rosette. For a very warm sound, move over to the other side of the soundhole, close to the fingerboard (this is termed playing *tasto*). For a hard, nasal sound, pluck close to the bridge (this is termed playing *ponticello*).

Compare the tone color of the following notes:

- string ② at fret 5

- string ④ at fret 14 (two frets higher than the point at which the guitar body meets the fingerboard)

- string ③ at fret 9

- string ① open

Apart from differences in tone color, what else do you notice?

Practicing

Daily Practice Routine

To get the most from your guitar study, it's important that you set up a *daily* practice routine. Musicians know from experience that it's far more effective to practice for a short time each day than to try to cram things into longer but more sporadic sessions. At the beginning of your studies you can achieve a lot with a well-organized daily session of 30-60 minutes. If you wish to practice more than this, split your practice into two sessions at different times during the day (rather than one long session).

Even more important than the time you spend practicing is the *way* you practice—ask any professional musician! Although entire books have been written about practice methods, for now use the following ideas to guide you in your approach to practicing:

- Form a clear idea about what you intend to play *before* actually playing it.

- Avoid practicing faster than you can think ahead—you should be able to mentally anticipate *(visualize)* each new action. In others words, *slow down!*

- *Repetition makes permanent*—don't repeat mistakes in the hope that they will eventually disappear. Instead, slow down and fix the problem.

- Practice and master short segments and put them together later rather than trying to practice an entire exercise in one go.

Warming Up

Playing the guitar is both a mental and a gymnastic activity and, like any gymnastic activity, it is important to spend a minute or two warming up before actually starting to play. An effective way to do this is to simply stretch the fingers, hands, wrists and shoulders before playing. Do this under the power of your muscles only (for example, don't use one hand to stretch out the other). After stretching, your fingers will feel loose, limber and ready to play. You should also stretch a little *after* practicing.

Counting Musical Time

A strong sense of musical time (the ability not to speed up or slow down, unless you really mean too) is one of the most important skills a musician needs to develop.

The first goal in developing your sense of musical time is to practice counting to a regular pulse or *beat* (you can think of pulse as the regularly recurring "tick-tock" of a clock, or the beat experienced walking or marching).

We count beats by grouping them into 2s, 3s or 4s. Each piece of music has a *time signature* at the beginning that tells us how to count time for that piece

"two-four time"　　　*"three-four time"*　　　*"four-four time"*

2 　　　　　　　**3** 　　　　　　　**4**
4 　　　　　　　**4** 　　　　　　　**4**

The upper number tells us whether we should count in 2s, 3s or 4s.

The most common time signature is 4/4 time, and this signature is often indicated simply by a "C" rather than by numbers (and is often referred to as "common time"). To count in 4/4 time, we simply count at a steady pace over and over in fours:

TRACK 02 | "1 - 2 - 3 - 4" | "1 - 2 - 3 - 4" | "1 - 2 - 3 - 4" | etc.

As you do this, counting out loud, you'll notice that the "1" feels stronger or more at home than the other beats. This is normal, and the "1" is actually referred to by musicians by a special name—the *downbeat.*

To count in 3/4 time we simply count over and over in groups of three:

TRACK 02 | "1 - 2 - 3" | "1 - 2 - 3" | "1 - 2 - 3" | "1 - 2 - 3" | etc.

And in 2/4 time, in groups of two:

TRACK 02 | "1 - 2" | "1 - 2" | "1 - 2" | "1 - 2" | "1 - 2" | "1 - 2" | etc.

It's important to practice counting musical time so you can later count mentally as you play without allowing the regularity of the pulse to waiver.

Rhythm Symbols

Of course, music does not consist of notes all of the same length. While some notes do last as long as a beat, others last for several beats (and some are shorter than a beat). Here are some of the symbols that are used to tell us how long a note should continue to sound:

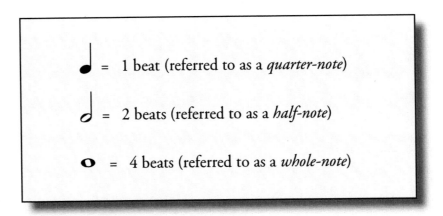

Counting Rhythms

To count the following whole-notes, establish the pulse by counting out loud in fours, tapping your leg each time you say "1" (Ex. 1):

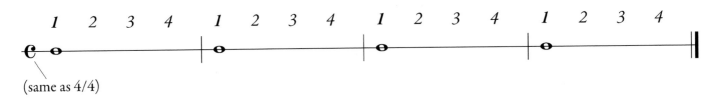

(same as 4/4)

Next, saying the "1" normally, practice whispering the "2," "3" and "4." This way, you reproduce the actual musical rhythm with your voice (Ex. 2):

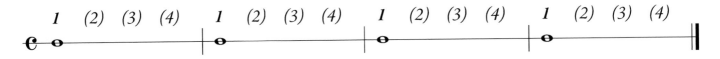

Next, we'll practice counting half-notes. Tap your leg each time you say "1" and each time you say "3" (Ex. 3):

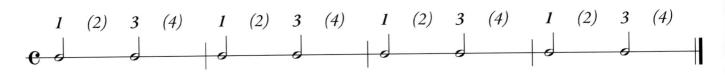

To reproduce the musical rhythm of the half-notes with your voice, count normally on "1" and "3" and whisper "2" and "4."

Counting quarter-notes is actually easier since you tap each time you say a number (Ex. 4):

Counting Mixed Note Values

To count mixed rhythms, simply use the appropriate count for each note value. Again, also practice whispering the beats on which no new note appears (Ex. 5):

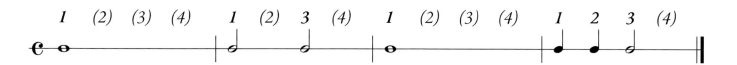

Here are some further examples for which you can work out and practice the counting (how is the final measure of No. 4 counted?) (Ex. 6):

Counting in 3/4 Time

So far, we've practiced counting rhythms that use notes of 1, 2 and 4 beats duration. But what about notes that are three beats long? A note of three beats duration is represented by a half-note plus a dot—the dot increases the duration of a note by half its original value:

$\vphantom{}$♩. = 3 beats (referred to as a *dotted-half-note*)

You can now practice counting in 3/4 time, counting out loud in threes instead of fours (Ex. 7]):

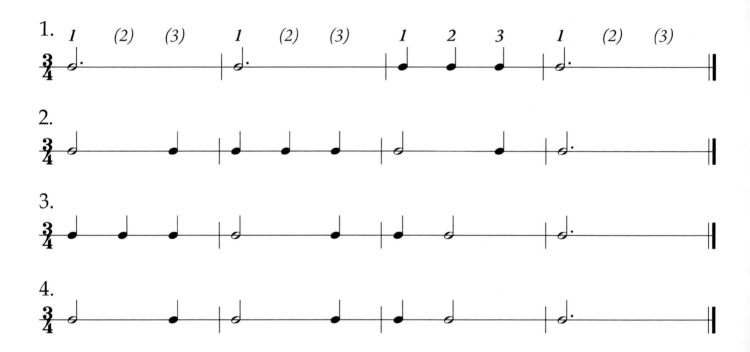

Using a Metronome

The metronome is a valuable tool that can help musicians develop their sense of musical time by providing a steady click or beep to play or count along with. Although it is still possible to find mechanical metronomes, digital metronomes are more reliable and flexible. Electronic metronomes also usually provide a tuning pitch you can use to help tune your guitar (see Tuning, next). Every musician owns a metronome.

Tuning the Guitar

Tuning is one of the most difficult things for the beginning guitarist to do. This is because tuning requires us to listen in a different way than usual. To tune an instrument we need to listen for the wavering sound that appears when two notes are not quite in tune with one another. The faster the wavering, the more out of tune are the two pitches. However, it can be difficult for a beginning musician to tell which of two notes is higher or lower in pitch.

Don't be deterred, help is at hand! Electronic tuners require no particular skill to use and models are manufactured specifically for guitarists. Of course, it's essential that you develop the ability to tune by ear, but at first you'll find an electronic tuner indispensable. Not only will your guitar always be in tune (which will help develop your musical ear), it will also be in tune with all other properly tuned instruments rather than merely with itself (and with the CD that accompanies this book).

There are, however, several methods of tuning the guitar without the aid of an electronic tuner, some more accurate than others. The first step is to get at least one string in tune by comparing it with an external reference pitch (from an electronic metronome, keyboard, pitch-fork, pitch-pipe, etc.). The remaining strings can then be tuned using this string as starting point.

The following chart shows how each string can be tuned to either of the strings next to it:

string ⑥ at fret 5 = string ⑤ open

string ⑤ at fret 5 = string ④ open

string ④ at fret 5 = string ③ open

string ③ at *fret 4* = string ② open

string ② at fret 5 = string ① open

Even if you're using an electronic tuner to tune your instrument (which is highly recommended), you should still experiment with the tuning method above to help develop the ability to tune by ear and use more accurate tuning methods later on.

Chords

To get started, we'll learn two easy chords on the three treble strings—C and G. The following version of the C chord is played by placing the first finger on string ② at fret 1 (keep all the non-playing left-hand fingers gently curled):

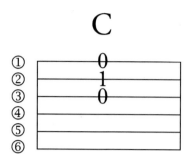

To make sure you're playing this chord correctly, check that you're using no more pressure than you really need to hold down the note, and check that all three strings are sounding clearly by plucking each one in turn with the thumb. Remember, you need only the three treble strings for this chord.

You're now ready to strum the three strings together. Place the right-hand thumb on string ③, keeping the other fingers naturally curled toward the palm of the hand. To strum through the strings simply move your arm from the elbow.

> Experiment by trying fast strums, slow strums, loud strums and soft strums, and by strumming at different points along the strings (near the bridge for a hard sound, over the soundhole for a warm sound, etc.).

Next, count out loud in 4/4 time, and strum the C chord in the following rhythm (Ex. 8):

TRACK 03

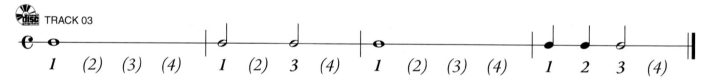

So far, you've strummed in a downward direction only. You can also strum with the back of the thumb in an upward direction, again moving only the arm from the elbow and keeping the fingers curled. In the following exercise up-strums are indicated with an arrow and have upwards-pointing note-stems; all others are down-strums (Ex. 9):

TRACK 03

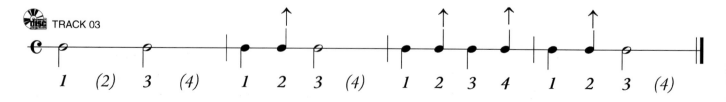

The G chord is played by placing the *fourth* finger on string ① at the *third* fret. Again, you need the three treble strings only for this chord:

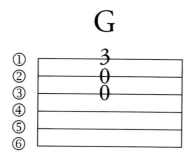

NOTE: be sure to use the *fourth* finger (not the *third* finger)—it's easy to confuse fret numbers and finger numbers.

Another Left-Hand Position

The left-hand position we've been using so far is referred to as a *parallel* hand position—since for most people the palm of the hand will normally be parallel to the fingerboard in order for the fingers to play on the same string, one finger per fret. When playing chords (and for playing in general in the lower positions) the arm is turned a little from the elbow (like turning a door handle or a key). This is referred to as a *rotated* hand position.

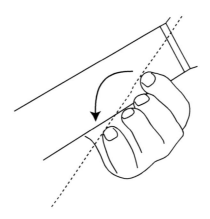

Changing Between the C and G Chords—Anticipating Left-Hand Movements

As a general rule, you should anticipate left-hand movements by placing the finger that will play next over its fret (or at least over its string) ahead of time. To prepare to change between the C and G chords, first establish a good hand position by placing the first and fourth fingers at the frets needed to play *both* chords:

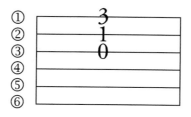

You're now ready to practice changing between the two chords. The goal is to make the transition as smooth as possible, without any break in sound. To do this, make sure the finger needed for each new chord is hovering over its string, ready to drop down, before you make the change. As you make the change, lift the current finger and at exactly the same time place the new finger on its string.

21

When you feel comfortable with this, play in rhythm and count out loud in 4/4 time as follows:

Here are two exercises to play as a duet with your teacher (or with the CD) (Ex. 10 & 11):

Music Notation

The Staff

Music is written on a five-line staff :

Each line and space on the staff represents a specific note (or *pitch*). Notes ascend on the staff from lower sounding pitches to higher sounding pitches:

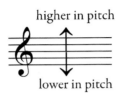

Ledger Lines

The lowest sounding notes (basses) on the guitar sound so low that they require extra *ledger lines* that temporarily extend the staff downwards:

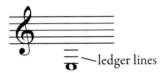

The highest notes on the guitar also require extra ledger lines, above the staff:

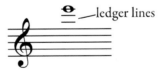

The Treble Clef

The symbol at the beginning of the staff is a *treble clef*—an ornate letter G:

If you look closely, you'll notice that the treble clef curls around the second line up from the bottom of the staff. This tells us that line represents the note G.

NOTE: Not all instruments use the treble clef; the bass guitar, for example, uses a bass clef: 𝄢

The Musical Alphabet

Musical notes are named alphabetically, using the letters A-G (if we ascend through the notes and reach the letter G, we start over again at the letter A for the next highest note).

Each line and space of the staff represents a particular note (or pitch):

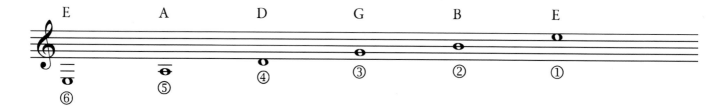

The guitar can play a lot more notes than those shown above, but we'll get to those later!

The Open Strings of the Guitar

Here are the positions on the staff of the notes produced by the open six strings of the guitar:

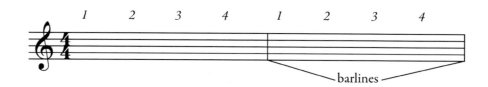

You should memorize these now (though we'll be going over them, and other notes we need, as we go along).

Barlines

The staff is divided into equal units of time (*measures* or *bars*) by visual guides called *barlines*. The note immediately following the barline is the "1" (or *downbeat*) that you have been counting in the earlier exercises:

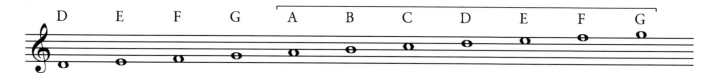

Repeat Signs, Double Barlines and Final Barlines

When a section of music is to be repeated, special barlines with dots are used, the end of a section of music is sometimes marked with a *double barline*; and the end of a piece of music is marked with a *final barline:*

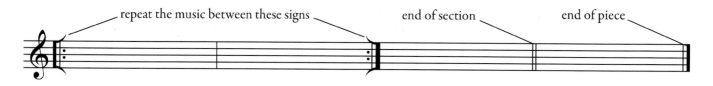

Plucking with the Thumb

The thumb is normally used to play notes on the three lowest strings (the bass strings).

To prepare to play with the thumb, gently curl the three right-hand fingers *(ima)* and lightly rest them on strings ③, ② and ① respectively to keep the hand steady. Avoid resting the little finger *(c)* on the sound-board—allow it to curl naturally and remain next to the ring finger *(a)*.

Place the thumb on string ⑥ and pluck the string, allowing the thumb to come to rest against the side of the *i* finger.

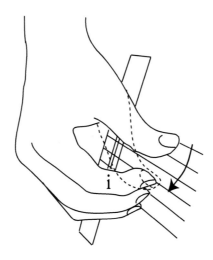

When you feel comfortable with this, you're ready to play in rhythm. Count out loud in 4/4 time, plucking the string as you say "1" and placing the thumb back on the string in preparation to play again as you say "4."

1 - 2 - 3 - 4	1 - 2 - 3 - 4	etc.
(pluck)	(prepare) (pluck)	(prepare)

Again, experiment with different sounds and degrees of loudness and softness by plucking at different points along the string and by plucking relatively louder or softer.

Here's the same thing written in music notation (Ex. 12):

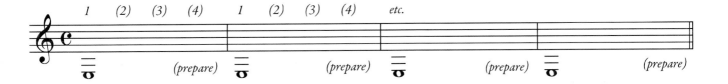

When this feels comfortable, repeat the exercise but instead of preparing the thumb on the string bring the thumb back *close to the string* ready to play again (don't actually touch the string before plucking it). This allows the note to continue sounding for its full value instead of being cut short by preparing the thumb on the string ahead of time.

You have now learned two ways of preparing the thumb to play its next note:

    1) by preparing *on the string*

    2) by preparing *close to the string*

Practice the same sequence of exercises on string ⑤ (A) (Ex. 13):

And on string ④ (D) (Ex. 14):

Here's an exercise on string ⑤ that practices the two types of preparing the thumb to play (the symbols in square brackets are *rests*—these are used in music notation to indicate silence) (Ex. 15):

In the following exercise, the thumb prepares close to the string only; there should be no silences (Ex. 16):

TRACK 06

Teacher / CD Accompaniment

If the thumb returns to the string very quickly, a *staccato* note results (the sound is cut very short). Intentional staccato notes are indicated by a dot *above* or *beneath* the note (Ex. 17):

Plucking Chords with the Thumb and Fingers

When playing chords (several strings played at the same time) with the thumb and fingers, the plucking action resembles closing the hand into a fist.

To get the hang of this, start out away from the guitar with your hand held in a gentle fist (the finger tips should be lightly touching the palm of the hand and the thumb should be held lightly against the side of the index finger).

To practice the plucking action, allow the fingers and thumb to relax out from the palm then quickly close the hand into a fist, lightly holding the fingers and thumb in that position. Relax out the fingers and thumb to return to the starting position (review the illustrations on page 9).

When this feels comfortable, transfer the movement to the guitar. Place the thumb on string ⑥ (or string ⑤ if it feels more comfortable) and the three fingers *ima* on strings ③, ② and ① respectively. Squeeze the strings a little and then pluck, bringing the fingers into contact with the palm of the hand. Here's the music notation for this:

Here are a few things to look out for:

- The little finger (*c*), although not actually plucking a string, should move into the hand along with the other fingers.

- All of the finger joints should curl in together (especially the main knuckle joint).

- Avoid bouncing the hand as you pluck—the movement should come from the fingers rather than the hand or arm (though the hand *will* move slightly when you pluck).

27

When this feel comfortable, moderate the plucking action so that the fingers come to rest inside the hand but not actually against the palm of the hand.

Next, we'll add some rhythm and explore just how the fingers return (seek out the strings) and prepare to play again. If we count slowly in 4/4 time, the sequence of events is as follows:

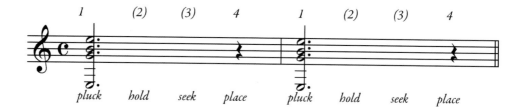

Pluck the strings as you say "1," **hold** the fingers in the hand as you say "2," relax the fingers and **seek** out the strings as you say "3," **place** the fingers on the strings ready to play again as you say "4."

Here it is in music notation:

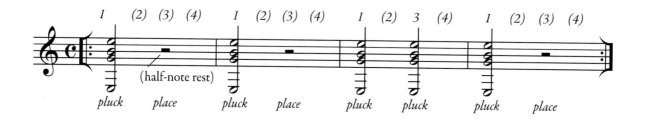

NOTE: the sign on beat four is a *quarter-note rest*, indicating the silence that results from placing the fingers back on the strings at that point.

When this feels comfortable, we can combine the **seek** and **place** phases into a single movement. Counting in 4/4 time, **pluck/hold** as you say "1" and **place** the fingers and thumb back on the strings as you say "3:"

In the following exercise, silences occur on the third beat of measures 1, 2 and 4 as the fingers are placed back on the strings (no silences should be heard in measure 3) (Ex. 18):

Alternating Between the Thumb and Fingers

Although we often play all the notes of a chord together as a "block," as we have been doing so far, it is also common for the fingers and thumb to play in alternation. In the following example, the thumb plays a bass string and is then followed by the three fingers (*ima*) playing the treble strings. Starting out with the thumb and the three fingers prepared on their strings, pluck the thumb as you say "1" and the fingers as you say "2," 3" and "4." To play this correctly, place the fingers back on their strings as the thumb plays its string (as you say "1") (Ex. 19):

In the following exercise, the thumb alternates between strings ⑥ and ⑤ (Ex. 20):

Review of Note Names

Here's a review of the six open-strings of the guitar and their positions on the staff:

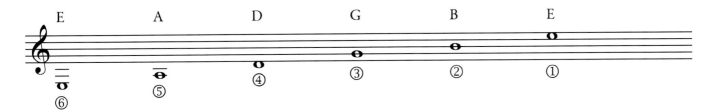

And here are some of the fretted notes that connect the open strings ①, ② and ③:

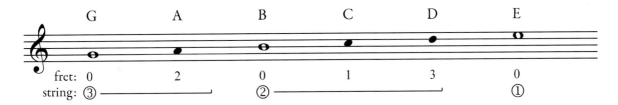

The following section, in which you'll learn four new chords, uses both tablature and standard music notation. However, you will now need to be able to recognize the notes from their position on the staff and you will need to know where to find them on the guitar.

Two New Chord Shapes—Am and Em

Here are two new three-string chord shapes you can use to practice some simple chord progressions. Make sure you understand how to decipher each chord shape from the standard musical notation as well as from the tablature.

As you practice each chord, pluck the strings one at a time with the thumb and check to make sure each note is sounding clearly. Also take care to use only the minimum finger pressure necessary to obtain clear notes.

[NOTE: remember, the numbers in the tablature represent *frets*; those in the musical notation represent *fingers*]

1. A-minor

The A-minor chord (usually abbreviated as "Am") is formed by placing the first finger on string 2 at fret 1 (the note C) and the second finger on string ③ at fret 2 (the note A). String ① (E) is played open:

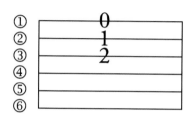

2. E-minor

The E-minor chord (Em) consists of the three open strings (E, B and G) only.

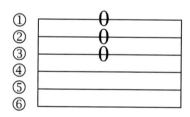

Changing Back and Forth Between the Two Chords

Once you've formed the Am chord you need only lift the fingers together, leaving the three strings open for the Em chord. Keeping the fingers hovering over the strings in the Am shape, it's simply a matter of putting the fingers down again to get back to the Am chord:

Am   Em   Am

30

When you feel comfortable with this, strum the chords in rhythm with your thumb and count out loud in 4/4 time as follows:

| 1 | - | 2 | - | 3 | - | 4 | \| 1 | - | 2 | - | 3 | - | 4 | \| etc. |
| strum | | strum | | strum | | (ready) | strum | | strum | | strum | | (ready) | |

Here's the same exercise written in music notation (Ex. 21):

Plucking with the Thumb and Fingers

Three-string chords are fine for strumming with the thumb, but for plucking with the thumb and fingers we need to add a bass-note to each chord (both are open bass strings):

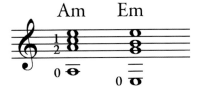

Practice the following patterns (Ex. 22):

Here's an exercise you can play as a duet with your teacher (or with the CD) (Ex. 23):

TRACK 08

Mazurka (slow Polish dance)

(repeat)

Teacher / CD Accompaniment

Accidentals—Sharp (♯), Flat (♭) and Natural (♮) Signs

We know that string ② has the note C at fret 1 and the note D at fret 3. But what about fret 2?

This is where sharps and flats come in. If a sharp sign (♯) is placed before a note, that note is raised by one fret. If a flat sign (♭) is placed before a note, it is lowered by one fret.

This is necessary because some notes of a musical scale are two frets apart (a *whole-step*) while others are only one fret apart (a *half-step*). Nevertheless, any note can be sharpened or flattened and it is then played one fret higher or lower than usual.

A natural sign (♮) cancels a previous sharp or flat and returns a note to its normal place.

Looking at string ② again, fret 2 can therefore be named both C♯ ("C-sharp") and D♭ ("D-flat")— they are simply different names for the same fret:

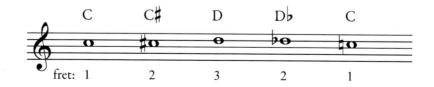

Another Chord—E-major

The E-major chord (usually abbreviated as "E") is formed by placing the first finger on string ③ at fret 1 (the note G♯). Strings ① and ② (E and B) are played open:

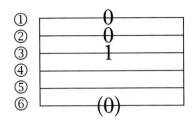 

Changing Between Am and E

This change is a bit trickier than the chord changes we've studied so far. You will need to lift the two fingers of the Am chord and move the first finger over from string ② to string ③ to form the E chord. To get back to the Am chord, put the second finger back on string ③ and, at the same time, move the first finger back over to string ②:

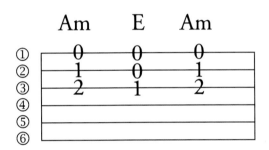

If you find this tricky, build up to the change from E to Am by practicing it in stages:

1. Leave the first finger down on string ③ and simply add the second finger at fret 2.

2. Place the second finger and at the same time lift the first finger from its fret.

3. Place the second finger and at the same time hover the first finger over string ②.

4. Finally, place the second finger and at the same time place the first finger on string ②.

This method of gradually adding movements one step at a time until you reach the complete change is a good way to practice any chord change that you might at first find difficult.

33

Here's another exercise you can play as a duet with your teacher (or with the CD) (Ex. 24):

TRACK 09

Pavan (Renaissance dance)

Teacher / CD Accompaniment

Another Chord—A-major

The A-major chord is formed by placing the third finger on string ② at fret 2 (C♯) and the second finger on string ③ also at fret 2 (A). The first string (E) is played open—a rotated hand position is essential for this chord (see p. 21):

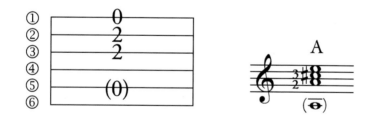

Adding Dynamics

In music, the term *dynamics* refers to playing with varying degrees of loudness or softness. When a passage is intended to be played loudly, it is marked *f (forte)*. When a passage is meant to be played softly, it is marked *p (piano)*. Normal volume is indicated by *mf (mezzo-forte)*.

Here's an exercise using the A and Em chords to play along with your teacher (or with the CD) (Ex. 25):

34

Sea Shanty (English sailor's work song)

Changing Between A and E

As you play the A chord, have the first finger ready, close to fret 1 on string ③. To get back to the A chord, position fingers 2 and 3 over their respective strings ready to switch out with the first finger. When switching back and forth between these chords, you can actually leave the first finger down the entire time:

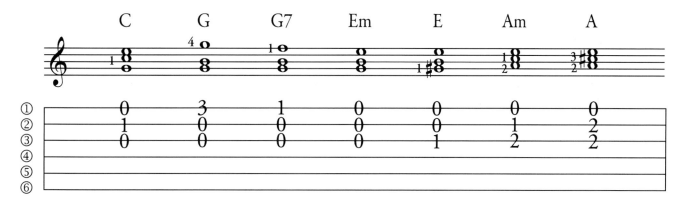

Chord Review

Here's a review of the three-string chords we've used so far, along with one new one—G7—which is played by placing finger 1 at the first fret on string ①. You should now have these chords memorized.

Here are a couple of new strumming patterns for you to practice using down-strums and up-strums. The up-strums point upwards and are marked by an arrow; all others are down-strums. Use any chord you like to practice these (Ex. 26):

TRACK 11

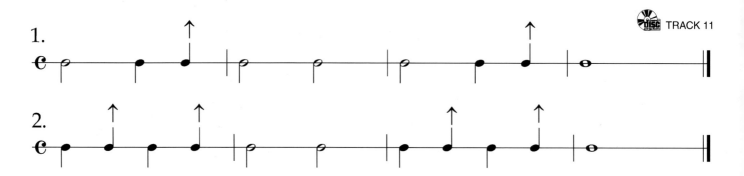

As you become comfortable with these, speed them up and add a rotating motion of the forearm to help you strum (a similar motion to turning a key in a lock). With this technique, one can alternate strums very quickly with hardly any up or down movement of the arm itself.

Chord Progressions

Here are three chord progressions that use the chords you've learned so far. Use any of the strumming rhythms you've practiced, and feel free to make up new ones if you like. If you find any of the chord changes tricky, use the method described on page 33 to practice them (and remember to anticipate the left-hand finger movements by placing the fingers over their strings ahead of time) (Ex. 27):

TRACK 12

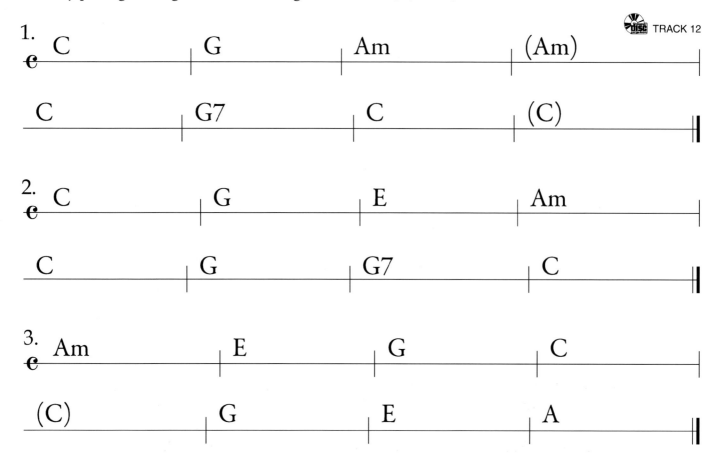

Using the Fingernails to Pluck the Strings

In order to obtain the maximum range of volume and tone color, classical guitarists use the right-hand fingernails to pluck the strings. This requires that the fingernails be carefully shaped, polished and looked after. Otherwise, the tone they produce can be quite harsh.

Nail Shape

Although guitarists eventually develop their own refinements to the shape and length of their nails—due to personal physical characteristics and tone preferences—it's best to start out with relatively short nails shaped to a gentle curve that follows the contour of the fingertip:

Notice that the curvature of the nail is quite shallow or "flat" and that the corners of the nail have been rounded-off but not filed down too low or too steeply. This approximate shape and length of the nail should allow the string to slide along the nail-edge quite easily.

Filing the Nails

The nails should be shaped with a particle-type metal nail file, rather than a serrated metal file, nail clippers or emery board. Simply place the *ima* fingers on the file in playing position and file them all together by moving the file along the nail-edges and fingertips and *gently* rounding-off the corners:

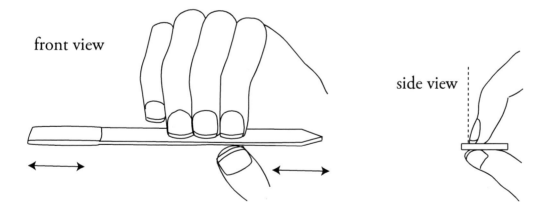

front view

side view

File the thumb nail separately, using a similar method.

To avoid harshness or "scratchiness" in the sound, the nail edge needs to be very smooth. To achieve this, always use a particle-type metal nail file and after filing polish the nail edge with the successively smoother surfaces of a supermarket nail buffer (or 600 or even 1200 grit automotive finishing paper).

NOTE: the left-hand fingernails should be kept short, otherwise it becomes impossible to fret with the tips of the fingers.

Placement on the String

Plucking with the nails requires a more precise placement of the fingers on the strings than using the finger-tips alone. After positioning the hand in the normal way (a relaxed fist with gently curved finger joints) both the fingertip and the left-hand corner of the nail should be in contact with the string:

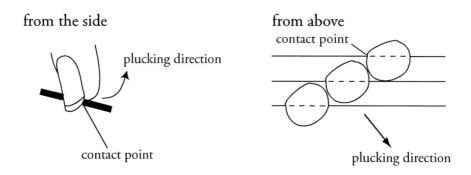

from the side   from above

plucking direction   contact point

contact point   plucking direction

Plucking Action

The correct plucking action is to simply close the finger into the palm of the hand, therefore plucking across the string at an angle (toward the elbow), as shown above. The string slides along the nail and releases somewhere toward the center of the nail as the finger moves through the string:

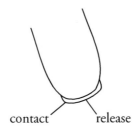

contact   release

Initially, when you practice plucking with the nails, allow the fingers to follow-through all the way into the palm of the hand (i.e., into a fist). Practice this with *ima* plucking together, on strings ③, ② and ① respectively, as well as with each finger plucking individually on its respective string. When plucking individual strings, at first allow all of the fingers to move into the palm along with the actual plucking finger itself. In all cases, rest the thumb on a bass string to help support the hand.

When this feels comfortable, moderate the plucking action so that the finger(s) come to rest inside the hand, but not actually resting against the palm.

The Thumb

The thumb works in a slightly different way than the fingers: the initial contact is with the fingertip and the *center* of the nail. The string then slides toward the corner of the nail as it is plucked (after plucking, the thumb should end up resting against the side of the *i* finger):

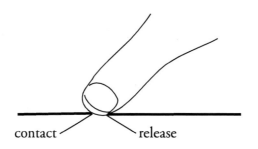

contact   release

Arpeggios

So far we've been strumming or plucking all of the notes of a chord together. A more common way of playing chords on the classical guitar is to pluck the strings individually in a recurring pattern. These patterns are called *arpeggios*. Arpeggios are one of the most important aspects of classical guitar music and playing technique.

The *p-i-m* arpeggio

Place the thumb *(p)*, index *(i)* and middle *(m)* fingers on strings ③, ② and ① respectively, squeeze and play the strings together a few times, then pluck in rhythm as follows (Ex. 28):

On beat four, all four fingers should be curled in toward the palm of the hand (though not actually resting against it) and the thumb should be lightly resting against the index finger. Although the ring and little *(a* and *c)* fingers do not actually pluck a string they too should move into the hand when the middle finger plays.

When this feels comfortable, practice returning the thumb and fingers to their strings as you say "4" (Ex. 29):

Finally, practice returning the thumb and fingers to their strings as you say "1" (that is, at the same time that the thumb plays its note) (Ex. 30):

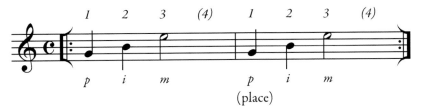

The *p-i-m-i* arpeggio

The *p-i-m-i* arpeggio adds the *i* finger at the end of the *p-i-m* arpeggio. First, practice returning the *i* finger to its string (Ex. 31):

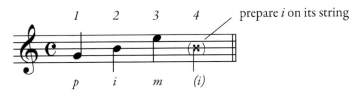

When you say "4," the *i* finger should be resting on its string ready to play again; the *m* finger should still be in the hand.

When this feels comfortable, play all four notes of the pattern (Ex. 32):

After plucking all the notes of the pattern, the fingers should be in toward the palm of the hand and the thumb should be lightly resting against the index finger.

Finally, practice returning the thumb and fingers to their strings as you say "1," as the thumb plays its note (Ex. 33):

Automating and Speeding up Arpeggios
An effective way of automating and speeding up arpeggio patterns is to alternate back and forth between playing the arpeggio slow and fast (Ex. 34):

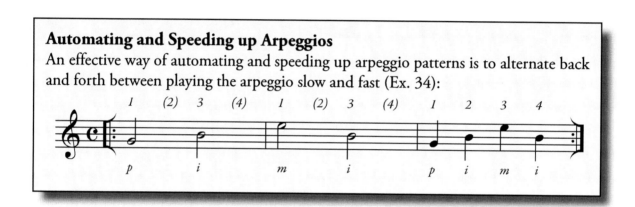

Combining the *p-i-m* and *p-i-m-i* patterns
The following exercise combines the two patterns we've studied so far. Prepare the fingers back on their strings as the thumb plays its note Ex. 35):

Here are four short studies that uses the *p-i-m* and *p-i-m-i* arpeggio patterns. Before playing each study as written, first practice the chord shapes (strumming with the thumb) and make sure you're comfortable changing between them:

Chord practice for *Arpeggio Study 1*:

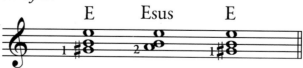

40

Arpeggio Study 1

Practice Arpeggio Studies 2, 3 and 4 in two ways: 1) with the repeats indicated; 2) without repeats.

Arpeggio Study 2

Arpeggio Study 3

The next study includes a slightly more challenging chord progression from Am to E to E7 to A (major). The E7 chord is formed by adding the fourth finger to an E chord (on string ② at fret 3) :

To change between E7 and A, be sure to place fingers 2 and 3 over their strings ahead of time. The goal is to lift the fingers needed for the E7 chord (1 and 4) and place the fingers needed for the A chord (2 and 3) at exactly the same time (you may wish to use the practice method described earlier on page 33).

41

Arpeggio Study 4

p   i   m   i   p   i   m   (etc.)

Studies 2 and 4 can be combined to make a longer piece:

Arpeggio Study 5

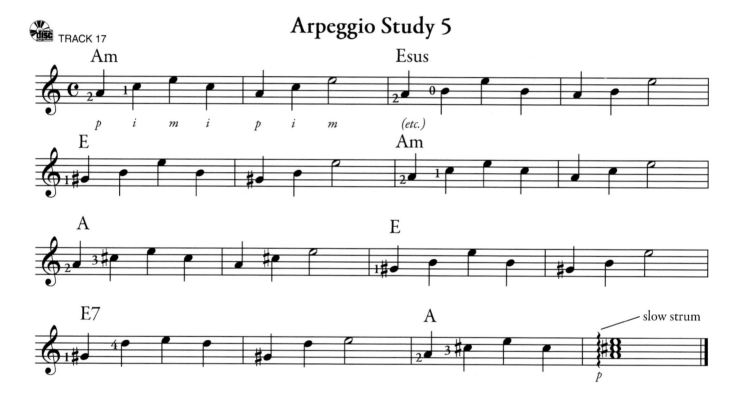

The *p-m-i* arpeggio

We'll learn the *p-m-i* arpeggio pattern using the same method we used for the *p-i-m* arpeggio. To begin, place the thumb *(p)*, index *(i)* and middle *(m)* fingers on their strings (③, ② and ① respectively) and play as follows (Ex. 36):

Again, after the three fingers have played their notes, the fingers should be curled inside the hand and the thumb should be lightly resting against the index finger. Also, don't forget to move the ring and little fingers into the hand when the middle finger plays.

Next, practice returning the thumb and fingers to their strings as you say "4" (Ex. 37):

Finally, practice returning the thumb and fingers to their strings as you say "1" (at the same time that the thumb plays its note) (Ex. 38):

Again, use the slow-fast practice method described earlier (on page 40) to help automate and speed up the arpeggio.

The *p-m-i-m* arpeggio

The *p-m-i-m* arpeggio adds the *m* finger at the end of the *p-m-i* arpeggio. First practice returning the *m* finger to its string (Ex. 39):

When you say "4" the *m* finger should be resting on its string ready to play again (the *i* finger should still be in the hand).

Next, play all four notes of the pattern. Again, after plucking all the notes, the fingers should be in toward the palm of the hand and the thumb should be lightly resting against the index finger (Ex. 40):

Finally, practice returning the thumb and fingers to their strings as you say "1," as the thumb plays its note. Again, you may wish to use the slow-fast practice method (described on page 40) to help automate and speed-up the arpeggio (Ex. 41):

Next, we'll combine the *p-m-i* and *p-m-i-m* patterns. Place the fingers back on their strings as the thumb plays (Ex. 42):

Here are two studies to help you practice the *p-m-i* and *p-m-i-m* arpeggio patterns (as before, practice the chord changes first). You'll need a new note, F♯ on string ① at fret 2:

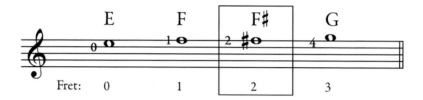

The curved dotted lines below are a reminder to leave down a finger common to successive chords:

TRACK 18

Arpeggio Study 6

TRACK 19

Arpeggio Study 7

44

Counting Eighth-Notes

So far all of our counting has involved notes that are at least a beat long. However, it's also possible to subdivide a beat into several shorter notes. Just as a half-note may be divided into two quarter-notes, a quarter-note may be subdivided into two *eighth-notes*. Eighth-notes are usually beamed together in pairs, fours or sixes:

NOTE: isolated single eighth-notes, however, are written with a *flag*. ♪ —more on this later.

To count the rhythm of eighth-notes, we subdivide the beat with the syllable "and," as follows (establish a steady pulse first):

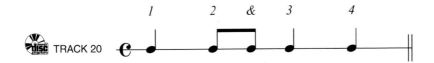

Use the following exercise to practice counting eighth-notes. Establish a steady beat before you begin and count the rhythm out loud (Ex. 43):

Eighth-Note Rests
Here's a review of the symbols used to represent eighth, quarter, half and whole-note rests:

45

Right-Hand Finger Alternation

Everything we've studied so far has been related to chords. To play melodies on the guitar we need to learn right-hand *alternation* technique. With this technique, the fingers pluck alternately on the same string (as well as from string-to-string, as we've been doing in the arpeggio studies).

To begin we'll practice alternating the *i* and *m* fingers on string ①. The finger action is similar to walking—as one finger plucks, the other finger comes back out of the hand ready to play.

Be sure to practice both *i-m* and *m-i* alternation, as indicated. Rest the thumb on string ⑤ or ⑥ to steady the hand (whichever is more comfortable) (Ex. 44):

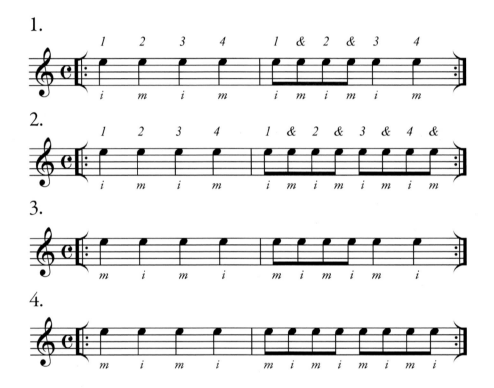

Automating and Speeding-Up Finger Alternation

Use the following practice method to help speed up your finger alternation: the fingers are placed on the string ahead of time, immediately after the previous finger has plucked its note. The result is a series of short *staccato* notes (Ex. 45):

Remember, though, this is a *practice technique* intended to help speed up your finger alternation and not the normal way to play—we should always strive to make our playing as smooth as possible, without any unwanted gaps in the sound as we move from note to note.

Next, practice alternating *a-m* and *m-a*. For most people this will not be as fast or as easy as *i-m* or *m-i* alternation, but it is important to develop control of the *a* finger (which will later be used to play the majority of melody notes on the first string) (Ex. 46):

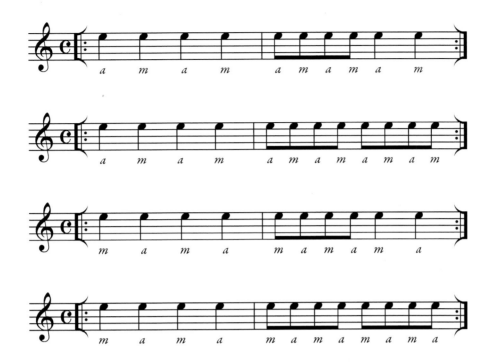

You may wish to use the staccato practice method just described (on page 46) to help speed up your alternation. *a-m* and *m-a* should also be practiced on string ②.

Single-String Melodies

Here are a couple of short melodies to play as a duet with your teacher (or with the CD). Use the rotated left-hand position you've been using for the previous sections and use strict right-hand finger alternation (using both *i-m* and *m-i* alternation). Also, try to make the movements of the left hand at exactly the same time as the right hand plucks the note to avoid unwanted gaps in the sound (smoothly connected playing of this type is referred to as *legato* playing) (Ex. 47 & 48):

TRACK 21

Third-String Melody

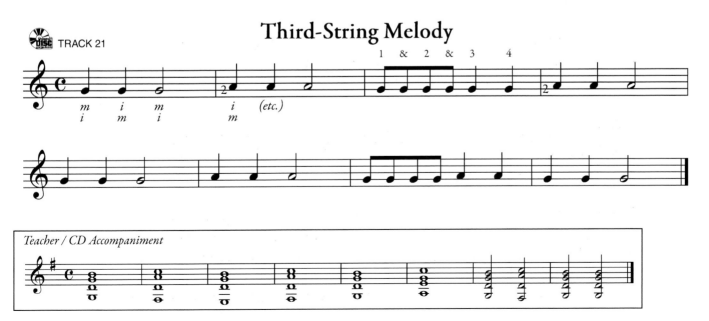

Second-String Melody

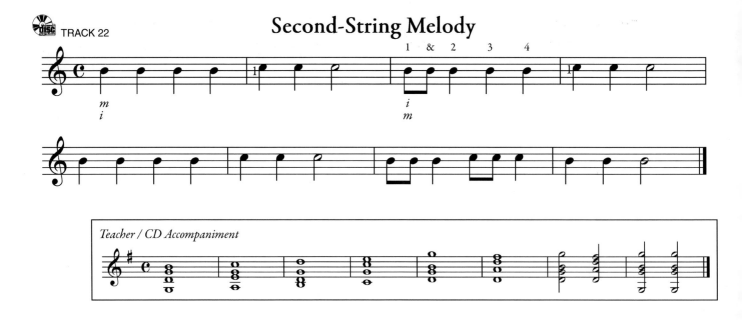

String Crossing

Next we'll practice finger alternation with string changes. Use the following exercises to practice switching between strings ② and ③ (Ex. 49):

To help make a string-change more secure, place the finger that is will make the string-change on its string ahead of time, as the previous finger plays: (Ex. 50):

Repeat the previous string-crossing exercises, preparing the string-changes ahead of time.

Next we'll practice some melodic fragments that move between strings ② and ③ (you may wish to practice the right-hand fingerings first), Again, coordinate the movements of the two hands as closely as you can and be sure to anticipate the left-hand finger movements by placing fingers over their strings ahead of time (Ex. 51):

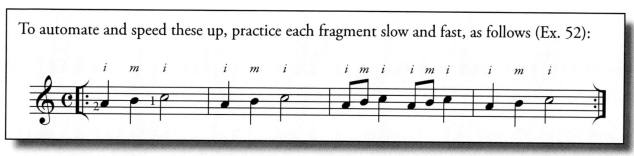

To automate and speed these up, practice each fragment slow and fast, as follows (Ex. 52):

Here are three short melodies based on the melodic fragments above to play as a duet with your teacher (or with the CD). Use strict right-hand finger alternation as indicated (it can be helpful to say the right-hand finger names out loud as you play) (Ex. 53-55):

TRACK 23

1. Walking

49

2. Skipping

The next melody includes two dotted half-notes—as mentioned earlier, the dot tells us to add an extra beat to the half-note, making it worth three counts (Ex. 55):

3. Dancing

The following melodic fragments use the second string only. Be sure to use the fourth finger to play D at fret 3 and practice with both strict *i-m* and *m-i* right-hand finger alternation (Ex. 56):

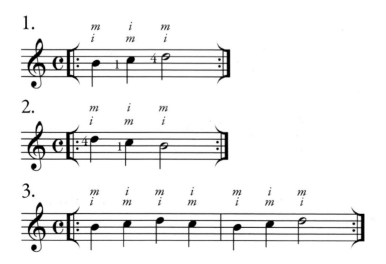

To help speed these up, practice switching between slow and fast versions of each fragment (as described on page 49).

Here's a melody that uses all the melodic fragments we've worked on so far, and which you can play as a duet with your teacher (or with the CD) (Ex. 57):

TRACK 26

Walking Further

Notes on the First String
The melody at the top of the next page is played on the first string, using the following notes:

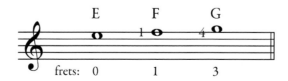

Again, be sure to use a rotated left-hand position, to use the fourth finger to play the G at fret 3, and to anticipate left-hand movements by keeping the fingers over the string (Ex. 58):

First-String Melody

"Good" and "Bad" String Crossings—Adding the Ring Finger *(a)*

You may have already noticed that some string crossings feel more comfortable than others, depending on the sequence of right-hand fingers used; when moving to a higher (thinner) string, *i* followed by *m* is more comfortable than *m* followed by *i*. Moving to a lower (thicker) string, the reverse is true:

Although it is necessary to be able to cross the strings using both "good" and "bad" finger pairs, it is often very helpful to incorporate the *a* finger to eliminate a "bad" one. The following right-hand patterns will help you smooth-out potentially "bad" crossings (Ex. 59):

Using Fingers Three and Four to Switch Strings at the Same Fret

When moving between two notes at the same fret on different strings we are no longer able to use the same left-hand finger for both notes—this would cut the first note short as the finger jumps across to the next string. The following exercise practices moving between fret 3 on strings ① (G) and ② (D):

Take care to use this fingering in the following melody whenever D on string ② is followed immediately by G on string ① (and vice versa); use the *a* finger in the spots indicated (Ex. 60):

Melody on Strings 1 and 2

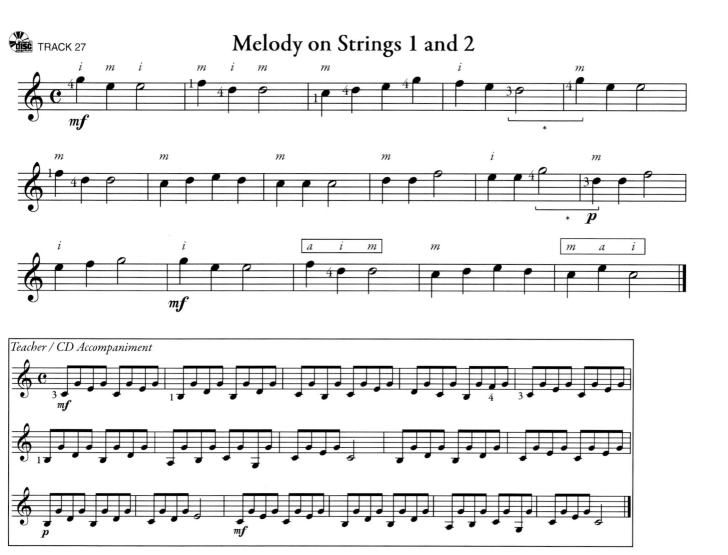

Dotted Notes

Earlier, we saw that a dot extends the duration of a half-note by one beat (to a total of three beats). Dots can be added to any note value, and this extends the duration of the note by one-half of its original length:

> ♩. = 2 beats plus one beat = 3 beats
>
> ♩. = 1 beat plus one-half beat = 1½ beats

When a single eighth-note appears alone (instead of in a group of two or more similar notes) it is written as a flagged note: ♪

A dotted-quarter-note followed by a single eighth-note is counted as follows:

Dotted-quarter-notes are used in the following well-known melody, Beethoven's "Ode to Joy" from his *Ninth Symphony*. The term **D.C.** at the and of the melody is the abbreviated form of the Italian term *da capo* ("to the head,") which means go back to the beginning of the piece and play again until you reach the word **Fine** ("end"). Take care to use the *a* finger at the points marked:

Pick-Up Measures

Not all melodies begin on the first beat of the measure. When a melody begins on some other beat, the measure is referred to as a *pick-up measure*. In the following example, the melody begins on beat four:

Usually, however, pick-up measures are written with the initial rests omitted:

Here's a famous melody from the Mozart opera, *The Magic Flute*:

O dolce contento

Wolfgang Amadeus MOZART

Keys and Key Signatures

When a melody uses the same altered notes *(accidentals)* throughout, a *key signature* is used at the beginning of each line of music. This tells us that certain notes will be altered (played sharp or flat) throughout the entire piece. There is then no need for accidentals to be provided each time an altered note is encountered:

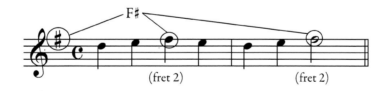

Key signatures are associated with the *key* of a piece—the note that a melody or piece of music is centered around and which the ear usually recognizes as the final note of a piece. Pieces with no key signature (pieces which use natural notes only) are usually in the key of C-major (or A-minor) and are therefore centered around the note C and the chord C (or, if the piece is in a minor key, the note A and the chord A-mi). Pieces with a key signature of one sharp are usually in the key of G-major (or E-minor). (We'll leave aside for now the theoretical explanation for this.) There are many possible keys (12 major and 12 minor) and we will be using several of them as we progress through this book.

Scales

Each major and minor key has an associated scale that presents the notes of the key arranged in stepwise order. Here's a G-major scale:

The following exercise uses all of the notes of the G-major scale (Ex. 61):

The following well-known melody, by the celebrated violin virtuoso Niccolo Paganini, is in the key of G-major. Take care to observe the key signature and to use the left-hand third finger at the point indicated and the *a* finger where indicated. Also, in the last two lines, the first finger (instead of the second finger) is used to fret A on the third-string (why?):

The Carnival of Venice

TRACK 32

Niccolo PAGANINI

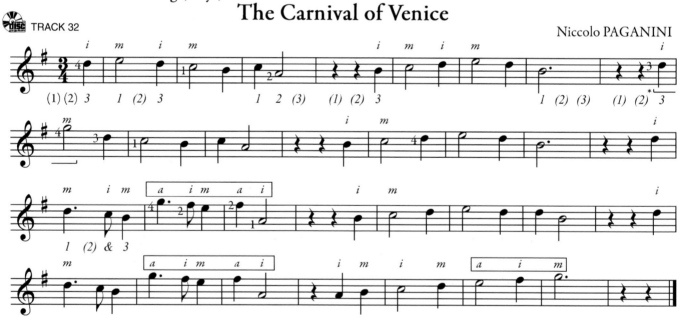

56

Review of Altered Notes

Since most of the melodies we've worked on so far have used natural notes only, here's a review of selected altered notes *(accidentals)* found on strings ①-③ in the first position (G♯, C♯ and F♯):

The following well-known melody by Franz Joseph Haydn is in the key of D-major and has a key signature of two sharps—F♯ and C♯. Each time you come across a C or F play them sharp. Since we will be playing on strings ① and ② at frets *two* and three (instead of frets *one* and three) we can use the third finger instead of the fourth finger at fret three:

St. Anthony Chorale

Franz Joseph HAYDN

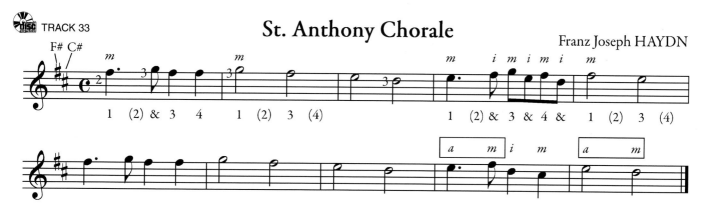

We'll finish this section with two scale studies in A-minor. To get these up to a decent speed, practice each measure separately, alternating slow and fast versions (as described earlier on p. 49). Then alternate slow and fast versions of each *pair* of measures. Each study should be practiced with both strict *i-m* and *m-i* finger alternation (Ex. 62):

Back to the Thumb

The following exercise explores the movement of the thumb over the three bass strings. Prepare the thumb on its new string ahead of time (at the points indicated) and rest the three fingers on the treble strings to help support the hand (Ex. 63):

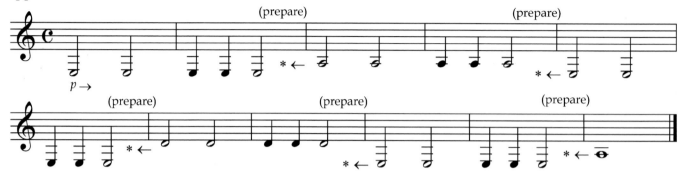

In the next exercise the thumb prepares on the new string only when time allows (at the points indicated). Otherwise, move the thumb to the new string and pluck as it arrives there. After playing the final note of the exercise, place the thumb on string ⑥ to silence it (Ex. 64):

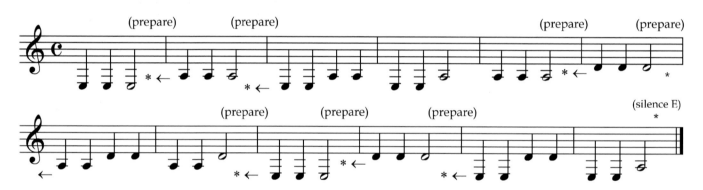

Here's another exercise for practicing the movement of the thumb over the bass strings. Prepare on the next string only at the point indicated. After playing the final note, quickly place the thumb back on string ④ and then on string ⑥ to silence those strings (leaving string ⑤ sounding for its written duration) (Ex. 65):

Notes on String Six

Here are the notes found on the sixth string. Use the third finger for fret 3 (fret numbers and finger numbers are therefore the same)—you will need to straighten the third finger a little and use a less rotated hand position:

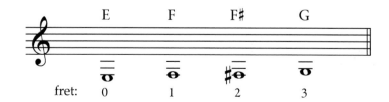

Use the following exercises to practice notes on the sixth string (Ex. 66):

TRACK 34

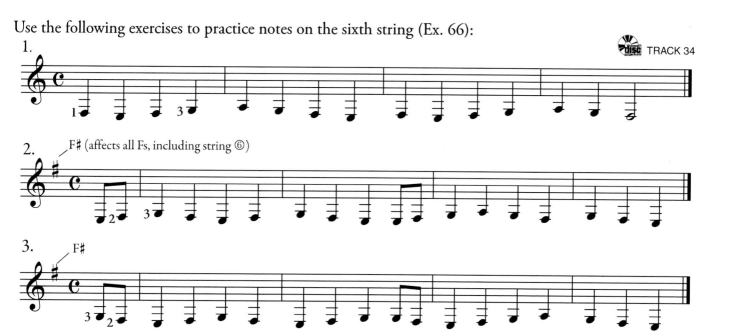

The following exercise combines the thumb playing across the bass strings with fretted notes on string ⑥. Be sure to keep each finger down until it needs to be lifted to play a new note (as indicated by the short slurs following the notes). The resulting effect is harp-like, all of the notes ringing over one another. The Italian term *lasciare vibrare (l.v.)* is sometimes used to describe this way of playing (Ex. 67):

TRACK 35

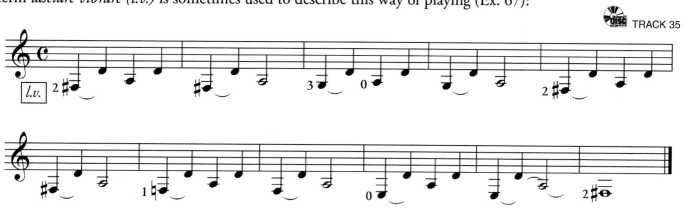

Notes on String Five
Here are the notes found on string ⑤. Again, use the third finger to play at fret 3:

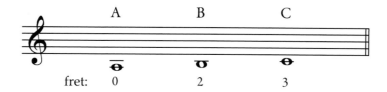

The following study uses fretted notes on string ⑤ along with the open fourth and sixth strings (Ex. 68):

TRACK 36

59

Notes on String Four

Here are the notes found on the fourth string (again, use the third finger for fret 3):

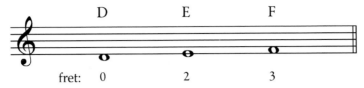

Here's a study for practicing the notes on the fourth string (Ex. 69):

TRACK 37

The following study uses fretted notes on strings ④ and ⑤. Be sure to keep the second finger down through-out the exercise (a *fixed finger*), as indicated by the dotted slurs (use the first finger to play B at fret 2 on string ⑤). Also be sure to keep the three fingers on the treble strings to help steady the hand (place them back on the strings after playing the chord at the end of the first line) (Ex. 70):

TRACK 38

Here's a well-known piece by J. S. Bach to play as a duet with your teacher (or with the CD):

TRACK 39

Minuet in G

J. S. BACH

Combining the Thumb and Fingers

When the thumb is busy playing the three bass strings, we normally use the *i* and *m* fingers to play any notes that may be needed on string ③.

Here's another well-known piece by J. S. Bach, originally written for the lute. You will need to use the fourth finger for the F on string ④ where marked (the C on string ⑤ would be cut short if the third finger was used for both notes). Practice the last two measures first.

TRACK 40

Bourrée

J. S. BACH

It is also normal to sometimes use the *i* and *m* fingers on the bass strings when there are too many notes for the thumb alone, especially on string ④. In the following piece, the *i* and *m* fingers are used on string ④ together with the thumb. Practice measures 5-6 separately. In addition, use finger 2 for the G where marked (again, to avoid jumping the third finger from string to string).

TRACK 41

Frère Jacque/Three Blind Mice

Review of Notes on String Five

Here's a review of the notes on the fifth string, along with a new note—B♭ (A♯), which is found at fret 1:

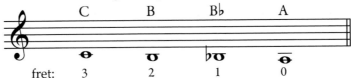

Use the following short study to practice B♭ and C on string ⑤. Again, in order to fret these notes with fingers 1 and 3 you will need to extend the reach of the third finger by straightening it a little and use a less rotated hand position (Ex. 71):

More Rests

The following study, by the celebrated nineteenth-century guitarist Mauro Giuliani, has several spots where you will need to use the thumb to silence a string (marked by the rests). Take care to use the specific left-hand fingering indicated at various points (to avoid jumping a finger from string to string):

TRACK 42

Maestoso

Mauro GIULIANI

The Alberti Bass

The following arpeggio pattern was very common during the classical period (c.1760-1820). Although it was used by almost all composers of the time, it is usually known by the name of one of the earliest composers to have used it, Domenico Alberti:

Polyphonic Notation

All of the music we've played so far has been written as a single line of music. However, since guitarists often play music that presents more than one line of music at the same time (for example, a melody with bass accompaniment) guitar music is usually notated *polyphonically*. In polyphonic notation, stems of different directions indicate the separate parts that are being played together. Writing the Alberti pattern in polyphonic notation we can see that the bass-line is presented more clearly and we get a better idea of how long the bass notes should continue to sound:

An Alberti Bass passage is used in the following piece, written by the famous nineteenth-century guitarist Fernando Sor:

Study No. 13

Fernando SOR

TRACK 43

Another Scale—C-major

Having learned the notes on the lower strings, we can now play a C-major scale. Here are two versions of the scale—the first uses the notes from C on string ⑤ to C on string ② (an *octave*); the second extends the range of the scale to include notes on string ① as well. *Notice that finger 3 is used to fret strings ④ and ⑤ while finger 4 is used on strings ① and ②*—maintain a rotated hand position, slightly straightening the third finger to fret the lower strings:

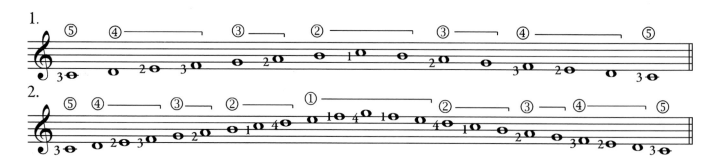

The following three exercises are based on the C-major scale. Practice these with strict *i-m* and *m-i* alternation throughout, even when playing strings ④ and ⑤ (Ex. 72):

Four-String Chords

Here are four-string versions of some of the three-string chords we learned earlier:

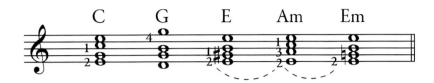

In the following two exercises, keep the right-hand fingers gently curved as usual (in normal playing position) but now play all down-strums with the *back of the fingernails*, rather than with the thumb. Up-strums are marked with arrows and should be played with the back of the thumbnail, as usual. If you have any trouble with the chord changes, use the practice method described earlier (on page 33) (Ex. 73):

TRACK 44

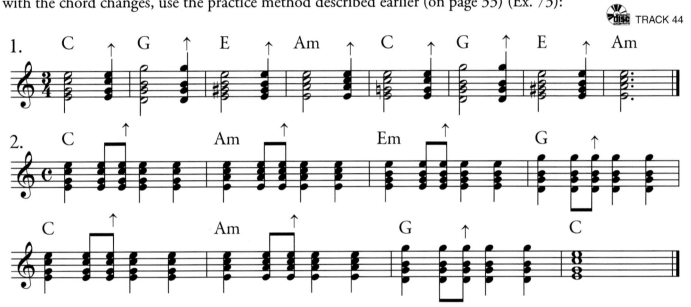

Here are four-string versions of the chords that can be used for plucking with the thumb and fingers together:

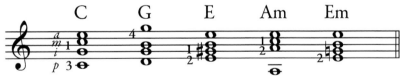

And here are two chord exercises to be plucked with the thumb and fingers. Be sure to let the bass-notes ring through the entire measure, whether open-strings or fretted notes (Ex. 74):

TRACK 45

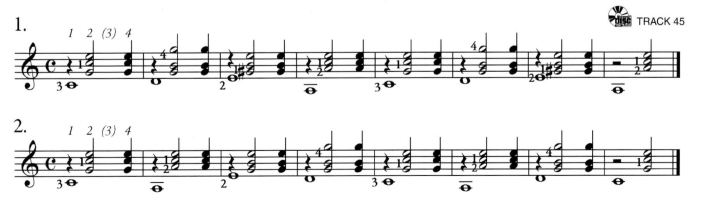

More Arpeggios

Arpeggios With the Fingers Only

The following arpeggio pattern uses the *a, m* and *i* fingers on strings ①, ② and ③. Rest the thumb on string ⑤ or ⑥ (whichever is more comfortable) to help support the hand (Ex. 75):

The following pieces are presented in polyphonic notation so the melody can be seen more clearly:

TRACK 46

Carillon (Bells)

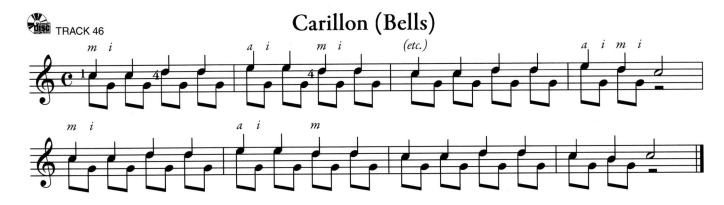

Here's a solo version of Beethoven's "Ode to Joy:"

TRACK 47

Ode to Joy (2)

Ludwig van BEETHOVEN

The *p-i-a* and *p-i-a-i* arpeggios

In the following arpeggio pattern, *p, i* and *a* play on strings ⑤, ③ and ① (Ex. 76):

The following exercise combines the *p-i-m-i* and *p-i-a-i* arpeggios: (Ex. 77)

Here's the same thing with the thumb switching between strings ④ and ⑤ (Ex. 78):

The following studies use both the *p-i-m-i* and *p-i-a-i* arpeggios. Be sure to anticipate left-hand finger movements wherever possible:

TRACK 48

Arpeggio Study in C (1)

In the following study, leave the third finger down as you change from measure 2 to measure 3 and add the fourth finger on the second beat of measure 3:

TRACK 49

Arpeggio Study in C (2)

Tied Notes

When two notes of the same pitch are connected by a curved line (a *tie*) the second note is not plucked. Instead, the first note continues to sound for the combined duration of both notes. In the following example, the C on the third beat of measure 1 continues to ring through measure 2 (for a total of 6 beats):

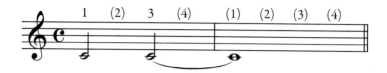

In the last two measures of the following study, C on string ⑤ continues to ring through the last measure (the *dotted* curved line is simply a reminder not to lift the first finger from the second string):

TRACK 50

Arpeggio Study in C (3)

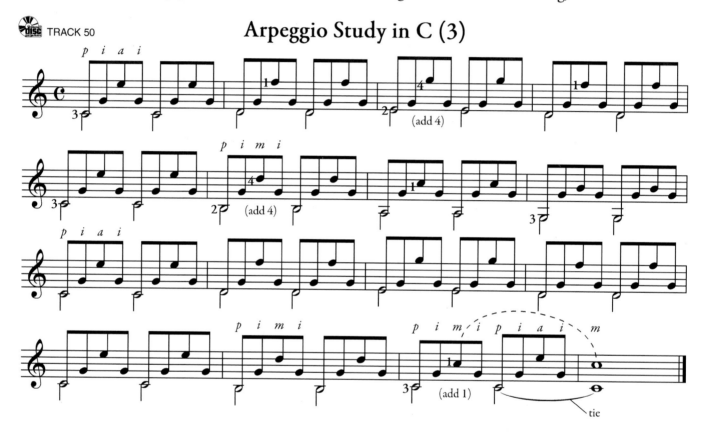

In the following study, *i* and *m* play on strings ① and ②; the thumb plays the bass strings:

TRACK 51

Arpeggio Study in A-minor (1)

68

Here's a common pattern that combines the *p-i-m-i* and *a-i-m-i* arpeggios (Ex. 79):

In the following study, the second fingers stays down throughout. Take care to leave down and add the other fingers at the points indicated:

TRACK 52

Arpeggio Study in E-minor

The final arpeggio study in this section is written in a common alternative style of polyphonic notation. The bass-notes are notated with their full duration (as whole-notes) while the upper voice at those points is notated with an eighth-note rest. However, these rests are merely *notational*, not actual silences:

Arpeggio Study in A-Minor (2)

TRACK 53

Accompanied Melodies

One of the most common types of classical guitar solo consists of a melody played by the fingers on the treble strings accompanied by a bass part played by the thumb on the lower strings.

The following melodies continue to use the *a* finger at key indicated points with otherwise strict *i-m* and *m-i* alternation. In addition, each piece focuses on one or two specific three-finger groupings.

The first melody is in the key of A-major (a key signature of three sharps)—all Cs and Fs in this piece are sharp (no Gs are used in this piece). The right-hand fingering patterns *m-i-a* and *i-m-a* are featured:

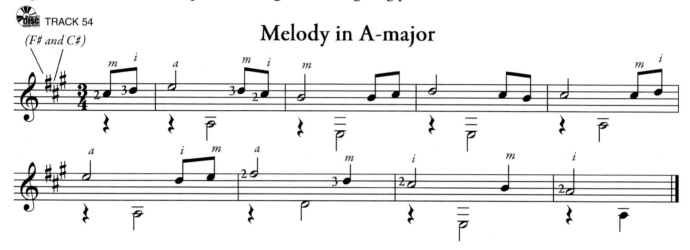

The following two melodies are in A-minor (no sharps or flats). The first of these features the right-hand fingering pattern *a-i-m:*

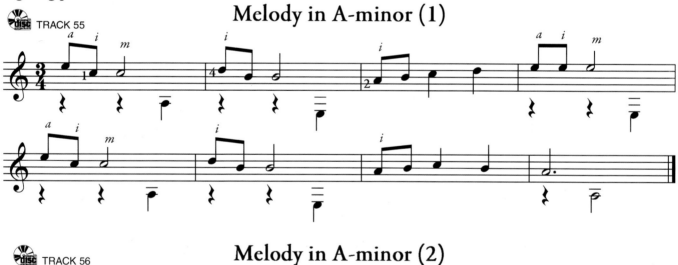

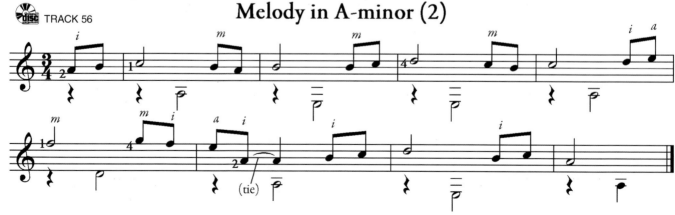

70

The following melody is in D-minor. Although the piece is notated with the correct key signature of one flat (B♭), the Bs in this particular piece are actually played natural and the Cs are all played sharp. Use the thumb for all down-stem notes, including those on string ③. The right-hand fingering patterns *i-a-m* and *a-i-m* are featured (it can be helpful to say the finger names out loud as you practice):

Melody in D-minor

Plucking With the Thumb and Fingers Simultaneously

In the following exercises, the thumb plays at the same time as a finger. Try to avoid unintentionally accenting a finger when the thumb plays at the same time. A good way to do this is to first play without the thumb and then focus your attention on the sound of the fingers only as you play the exercise, and then play the exercise again focussing your attention on the sound of the thumb (Ex. 80):

71

The following melody is in the key of A-major. All Cs, Fs and Gs are played sharp. The figure in measure 1 (and throughout) is played more easily with fingers 2 and 1 (as indicated) than with 3 and 2 (as would normally be used at those frets). The right-hand fingering pattern *a-m-i* is featured:

Folksong in A-major

Preparing the Left Hand for Playing in Two Parts

So far, most of the bass parts we've used to accompany melodies have used the open bass strings and these have alternated with the melody notes. The following exercises develop the left-hand positions needed for more independent bass parts in the keys of C-major and A-minor. The goal is to lift and place fingers at precisely the same time. Leave fingers down unless you absolutely must move them to play the next shape (Ex. 81):

The following study uses the left-hand movements practiced in the previous exercise:

Study in C-major

TRACK 59

Further Preparation for the Left Hand

The next set of left-hand exercises are a bit trickier—take your time with them! Once you've mastered these you will be ready to tackle many pieces of classical guitar music. Again, the goal is to lift and place fingers at precisely the same time and to leave fingers down unless they must be moved to play the next shape Ex. 82):

The following melody uses the left-hand movements practiced in the previous exercise:

Melody in C-major

Here's a variation on the previous melody. Use the right-hand fingering *a-m-i* throughout:

Variation (on Melody in C)

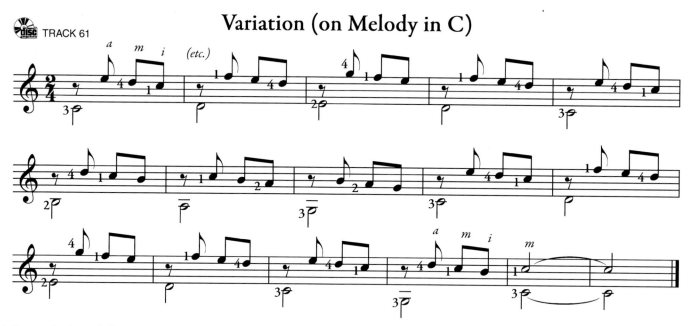

The right-hand fingering pattern *a-m-i* is also featured in the following melody:

Melody in A-minor(3)

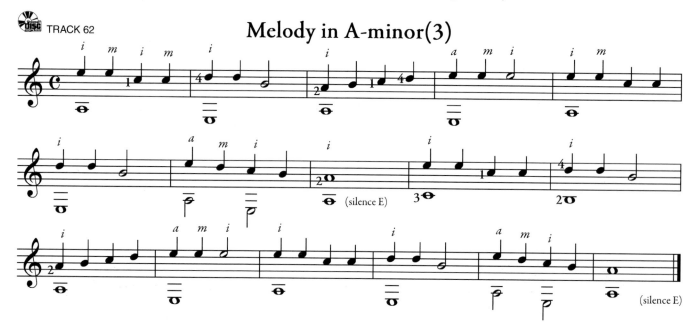

First and Second Endings

When a repeated section of music ends differently the second time through, special repeat bars known as *first* and *second-endings* are used. First time through, play the first-ending measure and take the repeat as usual. Second time through, however, ignore the first-ending measure and take the second-ending measure instead:

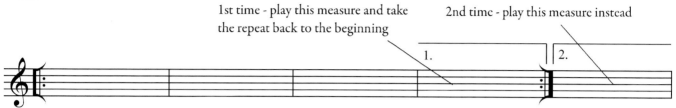

The following piece is based on an anonymous renaissance lute solo (Note: when a repeat sign leads back to the very beginning of a piece, the opening repeat sign is usually omitted):

A Toye - Renaissance Dance

Anonymous

A New Chord—D-major

The D-major chord requires three left-hand fingers:

The following strumming exercise uses the G, C and D chords, Again, use the backs of the fingernails for the down-strums and the back of the thumb nail for the up-strums (Ex. 83):

75

More Arpeggios—*p-i-ma-i* and *pam-i*

In the following arpeggio patterns, the *a* and *m* fingers pluck together (Ex. 84):

Here are two arpeggio studies that use the new patterns (Ex. 85):

Arpeggio Study in D-major

In the following study, be sure to anticipate the addition of the fourth finger to the E chord in measure 3 (Ex. 86):

Arpeggio Study in A-major

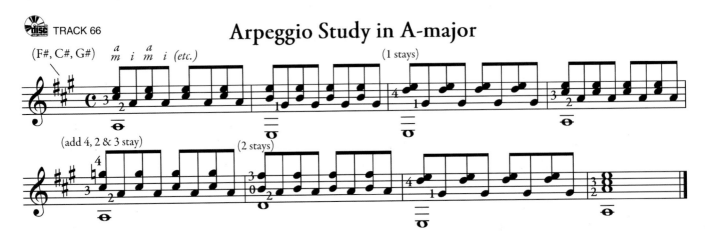

Daily Exercises

Now that we've increased the activity of the left-hand, we should take another look at the daily left-hand exercises you tried out at the beginning of this book (and that, hopefully, you've continued to experiment with).

Establish the position of the four left-hand fingers on string ④ in the fifth position (i.e., with finger 1 at fret 5 and the remaining fingers placed one per fret along the string—it can be helpful to establish the position by first placing the relatively weak fourth finger, and then work back to the first finger).

Next, practice adding and lifting fingers 2, 3 and 4 to and from the string *together* (as a unit). Finger 1 remains on the string throughout (Ex. 87):

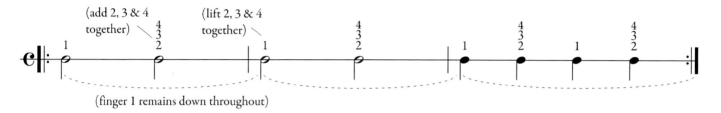

When this feels comfortable, develop the exercise by adding fingers individually. Beginning with finger 1 fretting its note and the other fingers hovering over the string, slowly place each successive finger until all four fingers are down on the string, as follows (Ex. 88):

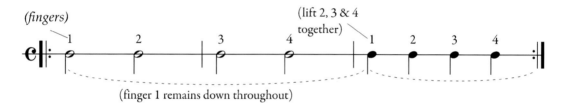

Here are a few things to look out for:

- Use a *parallel* rather than a *rotated* hand position.

- Keep the left-hand thumb relaxed, lightly resting against the guitar neck behind fingers 1 and 2.

- As you add each new finger, keep the previous finger *lightly* on the string—the sensation should be one of the finger pressure exchanging between the successive fingers.

- Once finger 4 has been added, and it's time to play finger 1 again, raise fingers 2, 3 and 4 from the string, leaving finger 1 in place to play again.

- Plucking each note with the thumb, try to make the left-hand movements at precisely the same time that you pluck the string.

For the next exercise, start with all four fingers down on the string and lift them off one at a time, starting with finger 4. When you reach finger 1 (which again remains on the string throughout the exercise), place fingers 2, 3 and 4 back on the string together as a unit, and start over again (Ex. 89):

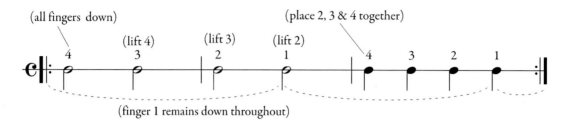

Practice these exercises for a few minutes each day, as part of your warm-up routine.

Daily Right-Hand Exercises

You should also regularly practice the various arpeggio patterns and finger-alternation exercises we've studied (using open strings). Rather than practicing all of them each day, we can divide them into smaller groups and practice one or two groups each day. I recommend you practice Group 1 daily and Groups 2 and 3 on alternate days. If you find this routine restrictive, at least try to go over Group 1 twice a week, and Groups 2 and 3 once a week. Once you become accustomed to the routine of technical practice, you'll find it takes only a few minutes to go through a group of exercises. Be sure to use the practice techniques described on pages 40, 46, 48 & 49, as appropriate):

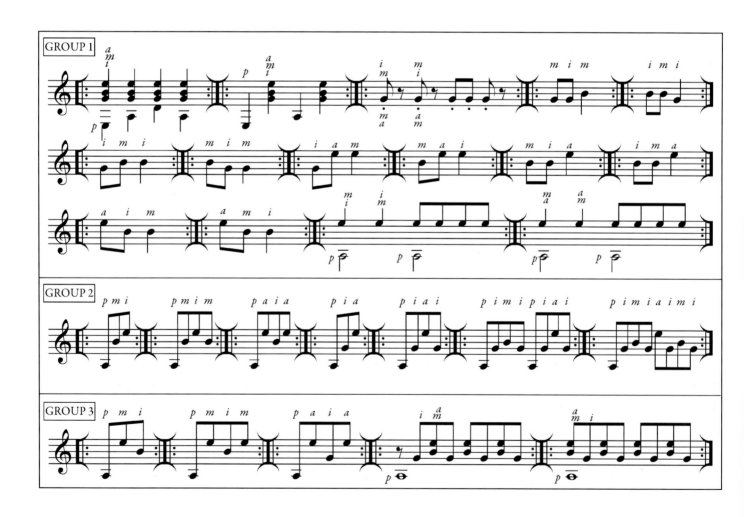

78

Pedal Point / *p-i* Alternation

A note that continues to be played throughout a passage is referred to as a *pedal* or *pedal point*. In the following piece—the popular Spanish folk dance known as *Malagueña*—the open first-string E provides a pedal to the bass-melody that moves beneath it. Use the *i* finger for the open E string and the thumb for all the other notes. Before working on the piece itself, practice the following *p-i* arpeggio fragments (Ex. 90):

TRACK 67

Malagueña

TRADITIONAL

Counting Sixteenth-Notes

In the same way that a quarter-note may be subdivided into two eighth-notes, an eighth-note may itself be subdivided into two *sixteenth-notes*. A quarter-note may therefore be subdivided into *four* sixteenth-notes. Sixteenth-notes have a double beam (or a double flag ♬) to distinguish them from eighth-notes, and are counted by using the syllables "e" and "a," as follows:

TRACK 68

79

The following piece is based on one of the most famous concert pieces of the entire guitar repertoire—Spanish composer Isaac Albéniz's *Leyenda* ("Legend"). The style of the piece is similar to *Malagueña*, above—except that in this piece the open E-string pedal is played by the *m* finger. Learn the bass-part first and, when this feels comfortable, add the *m* finger pedal. The notation for this piece uses eighth-notes for the bass and sixteenth-notes for the pedal (it isn't nearly as difficult to play as it looks!):

Leyenda

Isaac ALBENIZ

TRACK 69

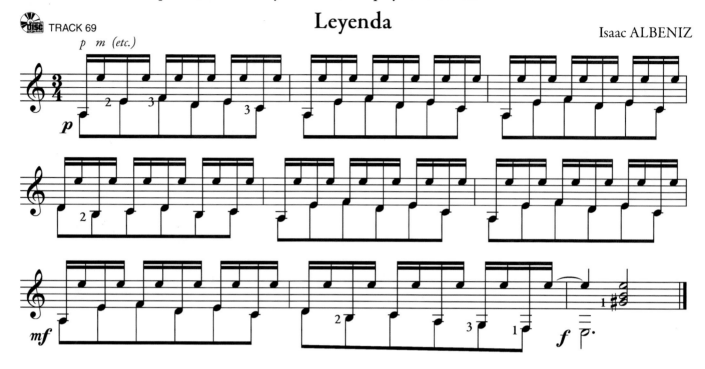

The Harmonic-Minor Scale

The following exotic-sounding scale is the *harmonic-minor* scale in the key of A:

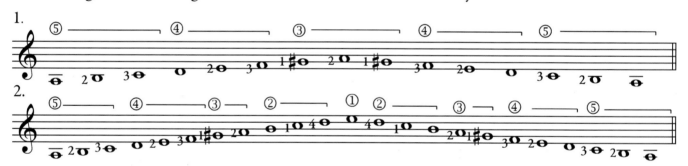

The following melody is based on the scale above and derives its "ethnic" sound from the unusual melodic interval F-natural to G-sharp:

Arabian Melody

TRACK 70

D♯ on the Second String—Position Shifting

D♯ is found on string ② at fret 4. To shift between this note and D♮ practice as follows: first fret D♮ at fret 3 with the fourth finger, as usual; then release the thumb from the guitar neck, relax the fourth finger so that it is resting lightly on the string and move the entire hand (including the thumb) to the next fret; replace the thumb on the guitar neck and fret the D♯ with the fourth finger as you arrive. The fingers should not change their curvature or positioning relative to the hand at all during this movement (Ex. 91):

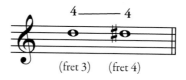

When returning to the normal position, again release the thumb from the guitar neck, relax the fourth finger, make the shift, and replace the thumb and fret the D♮ as you arrive there. Again, the fingers retain their curvature throughout the movement.

The following piece, Beethoven's famous piano melody *Für Elise*, uses this movement throughout:

Für Elise

TRACK 71

Ludwig van BEETHOVEN

Another Arpeggio Form—*a-p-m-p / a-p-i-p / m-p-i-p*

In the following arpeggio form the fingers alternate with the thumb, but unlike the arpeggios we've studied so far, the first note of the pattern is played by a finger rather than by the thumb (Ex. 92):

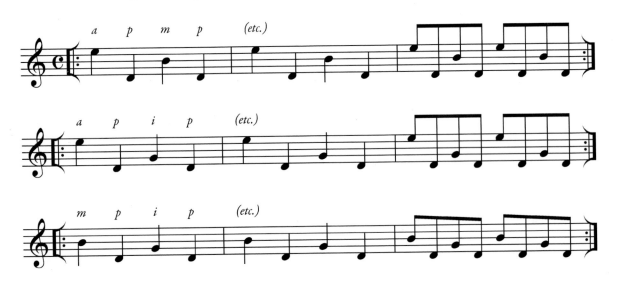

The following study uses the arpeggio forms just practiced. A slightly tricky chord change occurs at the beginning of line four. To switch from the previous chord, on beat one leave finger 2 down, take-off finger 3 and at the same time place finger 4. Follow this by adding finger 1 as you say "and". You should build up this change by practicing it in stages before working on the rest of the piece (see p. 33):

Arpeggio Study in D-minor

TRACK 72

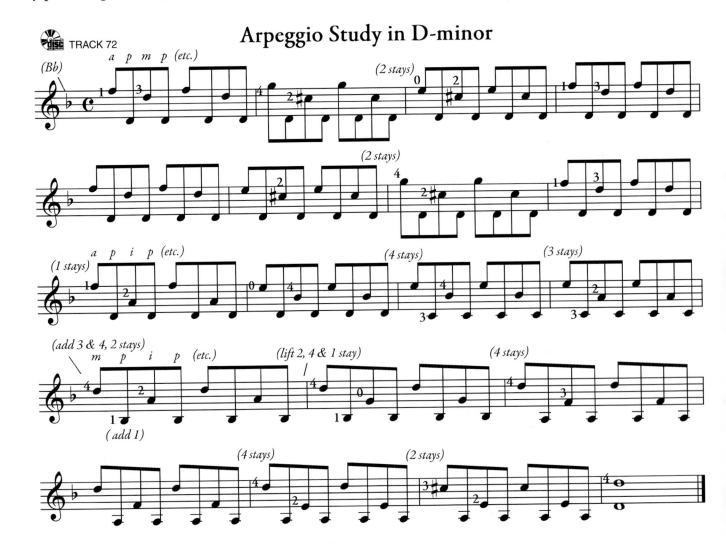

Arpeggio and Melody Combined

Often, the highest notes of an arpeggio pattern form a melody, accompanied by the other notes of the arpeggio:

Arpeggio Study in E-minor

Arpeggio Study in C-major

83

Compound Meter

So far, all of the music we've worked has been in 4/4, 3/4 or 2/4 time. In other words, the beat has always been a quarter note, and subdivisions of the beat have been into two eighth-notes (or four sixteenth notes).

In *compound meter* the beat is usually a dotted quarter-note, rather than a regular quarter-note, and the beat subdivides into 3s rather than 2s. The most common compound meter is 6/8 time. However, even though the upper number is a 6, we actually count only *2 beats* per measure. Think of 6/8 time as equivalent to 2/4 time, but with the beat subdividing into 3 eighth-notes, rather than 2 eighth-notes. We count subdivisions in 6/8 time by adding the syllables "and" and "a" as follows:

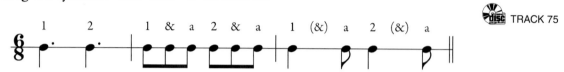

TRACK 75

Another way to think of 6/8 time is by comparing it with 3/4 time—one measure of 6/8 time works like two measures of 3/4 time. The main difference between the two is simply that the notes in 6/8 time go by more quickly (because of the speed at which we count the main beats):

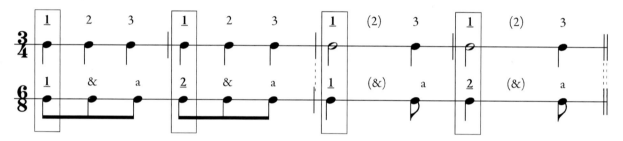

Here are two strumming exercise in 6/8 time, using the chords D, G and A. Use fingers 1 and 2 for the A chord rather than the more usual fingers 2 and 3—this allows finger 1 to remain in place when switching between the D and A chords. String ④ is played open throughout (Ex. 93 & 94):

TRACK 76

The strumming patterns and chord progressions just practiced are actually based on a Spanish dance form from the late 1600s known as *Canarios*. Spanish guitarists at this time strummed the basic chord progression to accompany dancing and played plucked versions of the chord progression with added melody lines to create solo pieces.

Here's a plucked version of the piece with some strumming at the beginning—play the down-strums on the first line with the back of the *i* fingernail only, using a simple flicking action of the finger—this allows the hand to stay in position for the plucked notes that follow (don't worry if you don't always manage to strum all four strings). Be sure to practice the counting indicated before actually working on the piece:

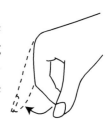

Canarios

SPANISH BAROQUE DANCE

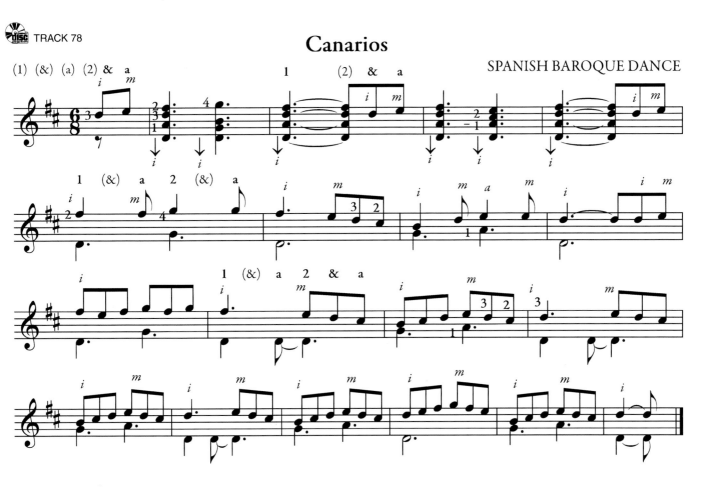

This brings us to the end of the first book of the *Mel Bay Modern Classical Guitar Method*. We've travelled a long way and I hope you've found it an enjoyable and rewarding experience.

On the remaining pages you'll find a review of the notes and chords used so far, an index of terms and techniques you should now know. I hope to see you again soon—in book 2 of the *Mel Bay Modern Classical Guitar Method!*

SY

Overview of Notes and Chords

Open Strings of the Guitar

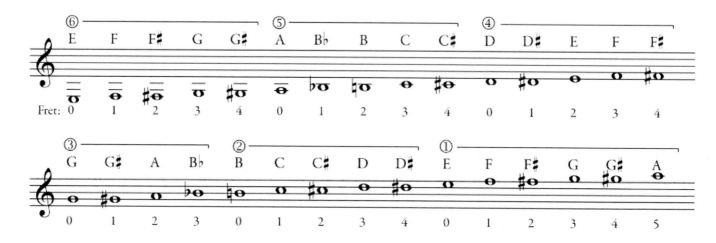

Notes in the First Position

Equivalent Sounds for Tuning

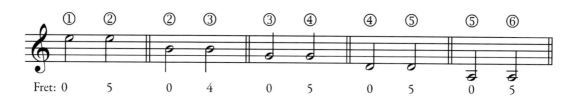

Chords for Strumming

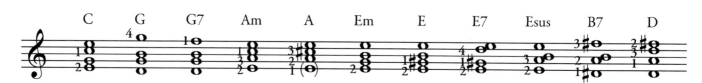

Chords for Plucking

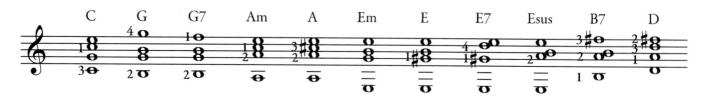

Terminology/Index

Stanley Yates

Stanley Yates enjoys an accomplished career as a virtuoso performer and recording artist, arranger, scholar, and teacher. Described as "one of an elite breed of guitarists" (Classical Guitar Magazine, England), praised for his "musical instinct and brilliant technique" (Suonare, Italy), noted for the "transcendent quality of his interpretations" (Fort Worth Star Telegram, USA), his performances, recordings and editions have been received with wide critical acclaim.

A past prize-winning performer in such prestigious competitions as the Myra Hess (London) and the Guitar Foundation of America, he is regularly invited to present concerts, masterclasses and lectures at leading music schools and festivals in both the United States and Europe. He has been dedicatee and/or first performer of music by such leading guitar composers as Stepán Rak, John Duarte and Angelo Gilardino, and has given first modern performances of such rediscovered works as the Premier Concerto by Ernest Shand and the Valsa Concerto by Heitor Villa-Lobos. His recordings for Reference Recordings, Heartdance Music and Aeolian Recordings include chamber music, his arrangements of the Bach Cello Suites, and premiere recordings of music by Mario Castelnuovo-Tedesco, John Rutter, and other contemporary composers.

His performance articles dealing with the music of such composers as J. S. Bach and Heitor Villa-Lobos have been published internationally, in six languages, in such journals as Il Fronimo, Gitarre & Laute, Gendai Guitar, 8 Sonoro, Soundboard and Classical Guitar.

He currently directs the guitar program at Austin Peay State University, home of Tennessee's Center of Excellence for the Creative Arts.